The Imprint of Alan Swallow

THE IMPRINT OF
ALAN
SWALLOW

QUALITY PUBLISHING
IN THE WEST

W. DALE NELSON

Foreword by Marilyn Auer

Syracuse University Press

Copyright © 2010 by W. Dale Nelson
Syracuse University Press, Syracuse, New York 13244-5290

All Rights Reserved

First Edition 2010
10 11 12 13 14 15   6 5 4 3 2 1

∞ The paper used in this publication meets the minimum
requirements of the American National Standard for Information
Sciences—Permanence of Paper for Printed Library Materials,
ANSI Z39.48-1992.

For a listing of books published and distributed by Syracuse University
Press, visit our Web site at SyracuseUniversityPress.syr.edu.

ISBN: 978-0-8156-0952-0

Library of Congress Cataloging-in-Publication Data
Nelson, W. Dale.
    The imprint of Alan Swallow : quality publishing in the West /
W. Dale Nelson ; foreword by Marilyn Auer. — 1st ed.
        p. cm.
    Includes bibliographical references (p. 197) and index.
    ISBN 978-0-8156-0952-0 (cloth : alk. paper)
    1. Swallow, Alan, 1915–1966.   2. Publishers and publishing—
Colorado—Denver—Biography.   I. Title.
    Z473.S95N45 2010
    070.5092—dc22   2010026330

Manufactured in the United States of America

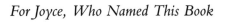

For Joyce, Who Named This Book

And I, who read and published words,
Worked warm within that marvelous air.
—Alan Swallow

All should be known about him, the great
and the not so great.
—Vardis Fisher

W. DALE NELSON spent forty years as a reporter for the Associated Press. During twenty years in Washington, he won the Aldo Beckman Award for excellence in reporting about the presidency. His poetry has appeared widely in general and literary magazines in the United States and Canada, and has been published in England and Australia. It has won awards from *Poetry Northwest, Plainsongs,* and *Visions,* among others. The author received a creative writing fellowship in poetry from the Wyoming Arts Council. His previous books published by Syracuse University Press are *The President Is at Camp David, Who Speaks for the President?* and *Gin Before Breakfast: The Dilemma of the Poet in the Newsroom.* He and his wife, Joyce Miller Nelson, a painter and writer, live in Laramie, Wyoming.

Contents

List of Illustrations   *xi*

Foreword, *Marilyn Auer*   *xiii*

Acknowledgments   *xxi*

1. A Bookish Youngster   *1*

2. Big Man on Campus   *24*

3. Down Altitudes of Air   *41*

4. Stern Critic   *60*

5. The Biggest City Around   *81*

6. Alan Swallow, Publisher   *102*

7. Alan Swallow and His Authors   *114*

8. Vardis   *123*

9. Expansion and Collapse   *131*

10. Postmortem   *155*

Notes   *173*

Bibliography   *197*

Index   *203*

Illustrations

1. Edgar Swallow Sr. as railroad worker   *2*

2. Edgar Swallow Sr. and bride   *4*

3. Powell's Main Street, 1923   *6*

4. Land on the Powell Flat   *7*

5. Alan Swallow and a favorite pet   *8*

6. Alan Swallow and sisters, Virginia and Vera   *10*

7. A view of Heart Mountain   *11*

8. Alan Swallow and father on family farm   *12*

9. Edgar Swallow pioneered in raising sheep   *13*

10. Lintel of Powell High School   *18*

11. Alan at high school graduation   *22*

12. Alan and Mae Swallow   *33*

13. University of Wyoming president Arthur G. Crane   *38*

14. At University of Wyoming commencement   *39*

15. Robert Penn Warren and fellow writer T. S. Stribling   *42*

16. On a Mississippi River ferry to cool off   *49*

17. Mae Swallow and daughter, Karen   *69*

18. Karen Swallow on second birthday   *70*

19. Edgar and Alan Swallow in uniform   *76*

20. The Swallows' house in Denver   *83*

21. Alan Swallow at work in study   *88*

22. Swallow and publishing partner Raymond Johnson   *93*

23. Yvor Winters and Janet Lewis   *105*

24. Alan Swallow and his Jaguar   *106*

25. The Swallows on a family picnic   *107*

26. Frank Waters   *116*

27. Vardis Fisher   *124*

28. Alan Swallow in 1960   *133*

Foreword

Marilyn Auer

Tom Auer, my brother and the founder/publisher of *The Bloomsbury Review,* was an avid book lover from the beginning of his life, as are all the members of our family. That love remains ever present in our lives.

As a teenager, Tom read voraciously and found wonderful writers few people had heard about. He encouraged those around him to read these extraordinary writers. In high school he started an underground newspaper called *For What It's Worth.* When he enrolled as an undergraduate at the University of Denver, he soon became editor of the *Clarion,* the campus newspaper. While at the university, Tom discovered the legacy of Alan Swallow, and his imagination was ignited. Swallow became Tom's mentor of sorts. As the years went by, it became clear that their lives had much in common, including spirit and intention.

To keep body and soul together during those college years, Tom found a night job at Bloomsbury Books & Pool, a local business that had the quality to be a successful independent bookstore, though most of the revenue in the early years came from the pool tables. Tom waited on the pool players and had plenty of time to read the books that lined one wall. This too was heaven. He found gifted writers and books that inspired and excited him, and he talked about them to customers. But few of these books sold. Tom realized that no one had heard about them because no one was reviewing them. He came up with the idea of starting a book review magazine that would review only new or underacknowledged authors. That magazine is *The Bloomsbury Review (TBR),* which began publication in 1980. We still publish the magazine with the same intent.

With a small group of family and friends and $5,000, Tom began building his dream, turning his love into his life's work, much as Swallow had done. He believed in people and their gifts, and he fought hard to offer a venue for their self-expression and talent. He had an open mind, an open heart, and a cool head. And Tom knew how to work, gracefully and graciously, under tremendous pressure. He was relentlessly creative in keeping *The Bloomsbury Review* alive.

Even as he did this, he pursued any and all information he could find about Alan Swallow, intending to write a biography tentatively called at one point *Alan Swallow: The Biggest Little Publisher in America.* Tom traveled around the United States to read the Swallow letters and archives at the University of Illinois at Chicago, Syracuse University, the University of California at Los Angeles, and other locations. He met or corresponded with Mae Swallow, Alan's widow; Karen Swallow, his daughter; Vera Swallow Cowel, his sister; and others. He collected and read many of more than four hundred books that Swallow published under different imprints during his lifetime. That list included works by Vardis Fisher, Thomas McGrath, Janet Lewis, Frederick Manfred, Anaïs Nin, Frank Waters, Allen Tate, and Yvor Winters.

In tandem with his working schedule at *TBR*, Tom attempted to set a writing schedule for the Swallow book. Up at four or five AM, strong coffee in hand, he would begin his day. That schedule came and went and came again. But he was dedicated and determined. In 1999 Tom was diagnosed with melanoma. His treatments were debilitating and his efforts Herculean. Tom died on April 18, 2003. He was fifty.

Alan Swallow died on November 24, 1966. He was fifty-one.

Before his death Tom was clear that he wanted someone to take on the Alan Swallow biography. And we found Dale Nelson, the perfect individual. Dale's reputation as a writer is sterling. He and his wife, Joyce, drove down from Laramie to Boulder to collect Tom's Swallow archive, drafts of chapters, and boxes of books relating to the project. Alan Bernhard, a dear friend, had done a miraculous job of converting ancient disks to ones better served by the twenty-first century. We loaded up the Nelsons' car and off they went, back to Laramie.

Though the book you are about to read is Dale's, it is appropriate to include a portion of Tom's draft for the preface of his book so the reader can hear Tom speak for himself.

TOM'S PREFACE

As far back as I can remember, I have always been enchanted by the printed word. From a very early age, books and magazines have provided countless hours of entertainment, learning experiences, and a lifetime of appreciation for what I have learned about from numerous printed pages. There are few things in my life that I have been quite so compelled to do as to read. It is more than a habit. It is a compulsion, and one I am thankful for having. One could have worse impulses, I tell myself. Suffice it to say that I count bookstores and libraries at the top of my list of favorite places to spend my time. They are wonderful sanctuaries where one can satisfy one's curiosity about many subjects, including the history of publishing, which also has always been of interest to me.

That is not the subject of this book, but it *is* the reason I happened to be snooping around the library at the University of Denver in the mid-1970s, looking for books about small presses in the Rocky Mountain states. And it is how I happened upon a slim, hardcover volume entitled *Publishing in the West: Alan Swallow,* edited by William F. Claire and published by The Lightning Tree, a small press in Santa Fe, New Mexico. That book, barely seventy pages long, contained tributes to a man I had never heard of by at least one writer I knew a little about—Anaïs Nin. It also included reprints of some of his letters to writers— Allen Tate, Richard Gillman, and Roger Hecht among them—and copies of a few newsletters that Swallow sent out to his writers, along with a list of more than four hundred books that he had published in his life, nearly singlehandedly, I would learn.

That book, and a newly born fascination with its subject, led me to another slightly peculiar volume that same day—a compact but hefty tome called *An Editor's Essays of*

Two Decades, written by Alan Swallow and published by the Experiment Press of Seattle and Denver. These essays included long, scholarly studies of writers I did not care much about—Sir Thomas Wyatt and John Skelton, among others—and several lengthy discussions about various literary philosophies and philosophers, again, not subjects I would, under other circumstances, find of much interest. But there was also a large selection of articles in this book that Swallow had written about writing and publishing in the West and about small presses and little magazines. Now *there* was something I thought I might enjoy. And I did. Frankly, it was not the writer's voice I found so appealing. Swallow's style of essay seemed stiff and formal and a little too academic for my taste. But what he wrote *about* and *how* he wrote about it, with uncommon passion and conviction and eagerness to educate—now *that* intrigued me. I was hooked. Here was a man I wanted to know more about.

Soon I would learn that Swallow had taught at the University of Denver, that he had helped start the creative writing program there (one of the first degreed writing programs in the country), that he had helped to found the short-lived University of Denver Press, and that he had later published hundreds of books out of his home, just a few blocks away from where I was reading about him. I also learned that he had died ten years before I had discovered him and his important work. As I read more by and about him, I thought, this man should be better known. And the more I learned about him, the more I felt like his contributions to literature and publishing in the West were far too important to be ignored.

The history of small presses is an especially colorful one, full of the exploits of rugged individualists who
thought they could publish at least as well as their peers
with better contacts or more resources. Oftentimes these
small companies and the people who have run them have
produced better books and more lasting or important
writing, and have published in greater effect than their
better capitalized counterparts. At the very least, it has
often been these small companies that have kept alive the
dreams of many young writers by providing an outlet for
their early work. A willingness to take a chance on an
unproven talent is one of the true benchmarks of the small
publisher.

Alan Swallow was one such literary legend whose
life and work deserves to be remembered as significant
in our publishing history, though he lived and worked
far from New York City. . . . At the peak of his career,
Swallow became known as "the biggest little publisher in
the West," a title that some found complimentary, others
slightly denigrating. It didn't bother Alan Swallow in the
least. He was proud of his small press and his little magazine. . . . In his mind, being called "little" was simply a
way of including him as part of an honorable tradition of
publications intending to reach a small, selective group of
readers—people who cared about literature. . . .

Perhaps more important than the four hundred titles
he produced in his regretfully short lifetime were the
threefold ideals that identified and kept alive his passion:
to publish what he considered good writing, whether or
not it had commercial potential; to keep that writing in
print; and to keep the cost of the books down to a level

that the average book reader could afford. He did so by doing most of the work himself. This was his publishing method. Swallow's lifelong devotion to his poets, fiction writers, and critics, and his ability to produce their work inexpensively, largely through his own labors, were to a great extent his greatest legacy. . . .

The list of Swallow's authors is a long one. Some became literary household names of their day, many were simply important western writers, many more were one-time book authors. All were important to Alan Swallow, singular voices who deserved to be noticed. And indeed, they might not have been noticed, were it not for the life and the labor and the love and the passion of one man, who "read and printed words" and "worked warm within that marvelous air."

This is his story.

Acknowledgments

S ave for Tom Auer," said the quick handwritten note that fluttered onto my bedside table as I opened one of the scores of scholarly books the late Thomas M. Auer had gathered in decades of research on the life of Alan Swallow. It was yet another reminder of the tremendous debt I owed to a man whose untimely death came before he could write the book he had labored on for so long.

This is not the book Tom Auer would have written, because no two writers will approach the same subject in exactly the same way. I can only hope that Mr. Auer would not have been too unhappy with the result.

Thanks also are due to:

The American Heritage Center, University of Wyoming, for a 1923 photo of Main Street in Powell, Wyoming.

The Center for Southwest Research, University Libraries, the University of New Mexico, for permission to quote from correspondence of Frank Waters.

The Louisiana State University Libraries for a photo of Robert Penn Warren and T. S. Stribling.

Grant Fisher for permission to quote from correspondence of his father, Vardis Fisher.

Grant Fisher and the Special Collections Department, Boise State University, for a photo of Vardis Fisher.

Cynthia Farah Haines for a photo of Frank Waters.

Jose Mercado of the Stanford News Service for a photo of Yvor Winters and Janet Lewis.

Photographer Joyce Miller Nelson for photos of Powell, Wyoming.

The University of North Dakota Library for permission to use brief excerpts from the correspondence of Thomas McGrath.

Karen Swallow for photos of her father, Alan Swallow, and other members of the Swallow family, and for permission to quote from Alan Swallow's poems.

Rowene Williams, director/curator of the Homestead Museum, for assistance to the author and to photographer Joyce Miller Nelson during a research visit to Powell, Wyoming.

The University of Wyoming for a photo of Arthur G. Clark, president of the university when Alan Swallow was a student.

Other acknowledgments are made in the source entries at the back of the book.

The Imprint of Alan Swallow

1

A Bookish Youngster

As a guard and detective for the Leadville, Colorado and Southern Railroad, Edgar Swallow was encountering tough duty. The trains took a wearying nine and a half hours to cover the 150 miles of narrow gauge track between the turn-of-the-century boom town of Denver and the red brick and sandstone station at the mining town of Leadville, also flourishing with the silver found in the black sand known as carbonate of lead. When he heard about a law passed by Congress in 1862 that made land available to any U.S. citizen and head of family who would live on the property for five years, turn it into a working farm, and pay the cost of reclamation, Edgar Swallow decided in 1909 to put railroad work behind him.[1]

It would be no easy task. The land available was just outside Powell, Wyoming, fifty miles from the Montana border in Wyoming's northwestern corner. He could file either at the Land Office in Lander, Wyoming, or in Powell. He filed at Lander, and took a full day's stagecoach and train trip over the mountains to Powell to see his land. It wasn't much to look at. No wonder they called it the Powell Flat, or just the Flat. In addition to sagebrush, cactus, and anthills, Powell was nothing but a collection

1. Edgar Swallow Sr., seated at right on a flatcar, had been a guard and detective for the Leadville, Colorado, and Southern Railroad. Photo courtesy of Karen Swallow.

of tents and one or two frame buildings. As Mrs. Charles Robinson, whose husband took her and their three children to the Flat in the fall of 1908, recalled, "I guess the thing that helped me from getting too discouraged was the train, which we could see from our farm. There were no trees and few buildings to hinder our view."[2]

Back in Denver, Edgar Swallow prepared to take his wife, Ida Kate, their young son Edgar Jr., and his two sisters north. As Swallow packed for the trip, his automatic pistol went off and he was shot in the stomach. He died a slow, painful death. Swallow had been a conscientious employee who always followed the rules by firing his weapon into a sand barrel when he left work. This time of all times, according to family tradition, he forgot to do it. A newspaper story suggested suicide, but this seemed an unlikely course for a man who was making plans for the future and doing something about them.[3]

At any rate, Ida Kate Swallow didn't have much choice. She was left with little but the children and an undeveloped homestead on the Flat. Ida Kate would become one of approximately 12 percent of homesteaders who were single women. Many of them, 58 percent by one contemporaneous account, failed and gave up their claims. Ida Kate did not. "I guess we'd better prove up on it," she said. She would stick it out for a lifetime, putting her among 22 percent who, according to one study, stayed on the land for a quarter century or more.[4]

By hard work and determination over the years, the Swallow clan would become successful farmers and leading figures in their community. One of them, Ida's grandson Alan, would have a career as a teacher, poet, and publisher that would take him far beyond the confines of Powell.

The arid regions of the Mountain West were about the only land left for planting under the Homestead Act. The fertile soil of the Midwest and the rain-soaked acreage along the Pacific Coast had already been grabbed up by would-be farmers.

Prospects improved when Congress passed the Reclamation Act of 1902, and $2.5 million was set aside for construction of a dam on Wyoming's Shoshone River that would water the needed land. The idea for such a dam had been first floated by the western showman and

2. Edgar Swallow Sr. and his bride, the former Ida
Kate Sayers, on November 14, 1887. He planned to
homestead in Wyoming in the first decade of the
twentieth century but died of an apparently acci-
dental gunshot wound before he could leave. Ida
Kate went in his place and homesteaded the land.
Photo courtesy of Karen Swallow.

entrepreneur William F. Cody, who called himself Buffalo
Bill, but his plan ran into money problems and the state of
Wyoming lobbied to have it built with federal funds. (In
1946, its name would be changed from Shoshone Dam to
Buffalo Bill Dam.) The dam was finished on January 15,
1910, a few months after Edgar Swallow's trip to Powell.

Now there was work to be done. Ida Kate and the
children moved from their poor Newton Street neighborhood in north Denver to Fort Collins and rented a house,
which she ran as a boarding house for students, across the
street from the Colorado College of Agriculture. The college, later to grow into Colorado State University, offered
a quick course in farming, and Ida Kate's fourteen-year-
old son, Edgar Jr., took to it with a will.[5]

In 1910 Edgar finished his course work and made the
move to Powell with his mother, now the head of the
family, and two sisters. The town they arrived in consisted
of a two-story Reclamation Service headquarters and a
few wooden buildings, fences, and dirt roads. It must have
been a letdown after the college town they left.

On the Flat, it wasn't easy, but Edgar Jr. had learned his
lesson well. On May 11, Ida Swallow applied for a water
right on seventy-eight acres of irrigable land.[6] Ten days
later, Edgar made a similar application covering sixty-two
acres. On June 23, another eight acres were added. In May
1917, seven years after the family arrived on the Flat, Ida
was granted fifty-three acres more.[7] On April 20, 1918, she
appeared before a U.S. commissioner and certified that
her homestead had been proved up as agreed.[8]

Crop yields were low at first, as the new farmland was
being brought into production. Lack of drainage in the

3. There were only a collection of tents and one or two frame buildings when Ida Kate arrived, but by 1917 Powell had a population of more than eight hundred. A photographer snapped this image of the town's main street in 1923. Photo from American Heritage Center, University of Wyoming.

early days of the irrigation project could turn farm fields into bogs.[9] To supplement the family's meager income, Edgar bailed hay and freighted supplies to the nearby Elk Basin oil fields. He hauled coal from the mines and lodgepole pine trunks, known as poles, from the mountains. As the work paid off, he expanded his acreage and before long felt himself well enough off to start a family.

On August 31, 1914, at the age of eighteen, he married Alta Helen Myers, a sixteen-year-old with an eighth grade education. Alta was one of the eight children of Lester Myers, a Baptist deacon and widower who moved in 1908 from a rented farm near Pleasantville, Iowa, to an eighty-

4. Powell, Wyoming, fifty miles from the Montana border, was sagebrush country known as the Powell Flat, or just the Flat, when Ida Kate Swallow first saw it in 1910. Lack of drainage often turned undeveloped farmland into bogs. This 1914 photo shows homestead buildings in the background. Photo courtesy of Karen Swallow.

acre homestead on the Flat. The Swallows' first child was born three months before Powell proudly graduated its first class of high school seniors. Edgar and Alta named their son Edgar Alan and called him by his middle name. Two daughters, Virginia and Vera, followed.[10]

The town Alan Swallow was born into began in 1906 as Camp Colter, the headquarters of the Shoshone Reclamation Project authorized by Congress and President Theodore Roosevelt. The camp was named for John

5. A Brownie camera caught young Alan frolicking with a favorite pet outside one of the farm buildings. Photo courtesy of Karen Swallow.

Colter, the veteran of the Lewis and Clark expedition who explored the area that would later become the nearby Yellowstone National Park. In 1910 the headquarters became an incorporated town and was renamed for John Wesley Powell, the American explorer, geologist, and irrigation expert. Unlike Colter, Powell had never been near the town that would bear his name.

Alan grew up on a homestead three miles from town, where his parents shared a house with his grandmother Ida. His father raised sheep as well as growing sugar beets, and by the time he was thirteen he and his sisters, Vera and Virginia, were given the job of caring for the "bum lambs," the ones who had lost their mother and needed to be fed from a baby bottle. Alan got to keep the money when he sold a lamb. There were other farm chores, and he later would ask readers to "picture the hard care with which he watered rows and fields of crops" in what was originally a desert.[11] From the fields west of Powell, they could see the eastern outcroppings of the Rocky Mountains, including Heart Mountain, which would be an internment camp for Japanese Americans while Alan Swallow was in an army uniform during World War II.

The boy's attention soon shifted from lambs to automobiles and motorcycles. The young Swallows didn't seem to have bothered with drivers' licenses. Vera, perhaps with a touch of exaggeration, recalled their "driving around the farm and town by the time we were ten." Alan bought a motorcycle with his lamb money and would "go out of the yard to see how fast he could go and make the corner and he'd tip over about as many times as he'd make it." One visitor saw him dipping from side to side on an oiled dirt road while driving no-handed. The children's father turned used-up Model T Fords over to them, and Alan tinkered with the machines, developing an early interest in engineering as a career. His father encouraged this activity, but his mother was dismayed by the motorcycle spills.[12]

6. Young Alan Swallow and his sisters, Virginia (right) and Vera, shared such chores as feeding lambs with a baby bottle after they had been separated from their mothers. Virginia died in 1945 at the age of 27. Photo courtesy of Karen Swallow.

The energetic youngster averaged a score of 77 out of a possible 100 in deportment during his six years at Powell Grade School, while his academic grades averaged 97 in spelling, 95 in history, 91 in geography, and 91 in

7. The Swallows could see Heart Mountain from the land they farmed outside Powell. Photo by Joyce Miller Nelson.

grammar. He was never tardy, and missed only one day of school. In "application," he was at first rated "good" and then "very good." He failed drawing in the second grade.[13] It was said that his parents could not get him to turn out the light at night, because if he wasn't reading he was writing. In the fields, he often walked by himself, whistling or singing as he went.[14]

Vera gave a vivid picture of life at the Swallow home: "I remember the gasoline lamps, the kerosene lights, the lamp chimneys to clean, the house so cold in the mornings, the wood burning stoves, the wonderful scent of fresh bread and cinnamon rolls, the baby chicks behind the stove in the Spring . . . ordered by mail, and shipped through the post office, and sometimes the tiny lambs behind the stove." She and Virginia each had two

8. Edgar Swallow and his son took a break from work on the family farm outside Powell, Wyoming. Photo courtesy of Karen Swallow.

dresses, "one for school and one for everyday," and always changed after school so they could wear both dresses for a week. Edgar Swallow Jr. was soon thriving as a farmer and rising as a leader in the community. To counter the

9. Beet growing was not paying off very well, and Edgar urged other farmers to join him in diversifying by raising sheep. Photo courtesy of Karen Swallow.

disappointing crop yields, he encouraged less enterprising farmers to diversify, investing in sheep that they would graze in the hills in the summer and feed on the farm in the winter. Sometimes he bought the lambs and sold them to reluctant farmers who "in the winter . . . just went to town and sat around in the pool hall; there was nothing to do," Vera recalled.[15]

At home Edgar was the talker in the family; Alta was quiet. One visitor to the home described Edgar as "a big kidder" and "a rolling force over everyone." To his children, he was not stern. Religion did not play a big role in the family's life. Edgar attended the Union Presbyterian church only on Easter and other special occasions and once leaned over in a pew to observe that the two biggest crooks in town were taking up the collection. The family visited Yellowstone Park every summer, staying in a rented cabin on the North Fork of the Shoshone River. Once, on the way to the park, he was allowing the underage and speed-crazy Alan to drive his Model A Ford when he spotted a patrol car. "Move over; let me in the driver's seat," he said. To Vera in the backseat, he said,

"You keep quiet." The son was speeding, but the father got the ticket.

Alan was a bookish youngster. One unconfirmed story had him driving a tractor into the barn while reading. Vera said she didn't see this happen, but didn't doubt it; "I just don't recall him, as a boy, doing anything without a book in his face."[16] In his teens, he clipped articles from *Good Housekeeping* and *The American,* magazines his parents subscribed to, about such popular authors of the day as poets Edwin Markham and Edna St. Vincent Millay, as well as the obituary in 1931 of the poet Vachel Lindsay. Over an admiring article on a high church official's description of popular crooners as making "the basest appeal to sex emotions in the young," he wrote, "Bunk."[17]

Alan may have been much like the boy, "at least as young as eleven," whom, after he began writing books himself, he described in a story called "Golden Girl": a boy who dreamed of meeting his love "in the clear, white dangers of the crystalline blizzard" that so often surrounded him, and leading her to the warmth of his embraces.[18]

It was his mechanical skills, not his erotic dreams, however, that got him a summer job. In 1931, when he was sixteen and between his junior and senior years in high school, he went to work for the operators of a tourist business in Gardiner, Montana, just outside the north entrance to Yellowstone National Park. The business occupied two buildings, the larger housing a grocery store and soda fountain and the smaller a filling station, as automobile service stations were then known.

The Swallow family drove up from Powell that summer to see how Alan was getting along. He was getting along fine. His job was to run the filling station from 6:00 in the morning to 8:00 or 8:30 at night. He was paid $65 per month plus his room and board. The tourists came by in rushes, thirty minutes or so at a time, with intervals of up to half an hour in between when Alan had time to read. Years later he was to recall that there was not a bookstore in the entire state of Wyoming, and few if any in Montana.[19] His reading had been largely confined to magazines and to books on mechanical subjects. But somewhere in Gardiner he discovered Emanuel Haldeman-Julius, and the discovery would affect the course of his life.

Haldeman-Julius, born Emanuel Julius in 1889 in a Philadelphia tenement, had a passion for books that he shared with his Russian immigrant father, a bookbinder by trade.[20] Haldeman-Julius first gained notice as a Socialist newspaper editor and writer of antireligious tracts. Most important to Alan Swallow, however, he became the publisher of the Little Blue Books. He had been marketing these books from his publishing firm in Gerard, Kansas, a town of three thousand population, since 1919. Then he bought the press of the Socialist newspaper *The Appeal to Reason* with $75,000 borrowed from his wife, Marcet Haldeman. At that time he prefixed the name Haldeman to his own.[21]

The would-be publisher's next decision was what to publish. It wasn't hard. He had been "lifted out of this world" at the age of fifteen when he sat on a park bench on a chilly Philadelphia day and read Oscar Wilde's "Ballad of Reading Gaol" straight through. He judged manuscripts, he said, "by only one standard—do I like it?" He liked the Wilde poem. He also liked *The Rubaiyat of Omar Khayyam* in the Edward Fitzgerald translation. They were his first choices, priced at twenty-five cents a copy. By the 1920s he had lowered his prices to five cents apiece for such works as Shelley's *A Defense of Poetry,* a biography of Thomas Edison, *Woman's Sexual Life,* and *Catholicism and Sex.*

Haldeman-Julius wasn't above sharp practice, sometimes advertising that customers had better buy now because the price of the books was going up. The price didn't go up, but the publisher profited from the increased sales.[22] Alan figured he probably bought 250 of the books. He had a lot of company. Charlie Chaplin and Ethiopian Emperor Haile Selassie bought them; Admiral Richard Byrd took 1,500 on his expedition to the South Pole.[23]

Alan Swallow formed two convictions. One was that he wanted to be a poet, and he wrote his first poems that summer in Gardiner. Second, if a Jew from a Philadelphia slum could publish books in Gerard, Kansas, there might be a chance for a boy from the Flat to become a publisher also. While New York and Boston dominated the publishing scene, small-town publishers were not unknown. Caxton Printers of Caldwell, Idaho, later to call its publishing arm Caxton Press, began commercial publishing in 1927.

Reading books and fixing engines were not Alan's only preoccupations that summer. In a sketch he wrote in 1933, beginning "I wish I were young" (he was eighteen at the time), he described "a beautiful night" in Gardiner when he fell in with a slightly drunk young transient from New York with whom he talked "under the close intimacy of the night." His companion talked of visiting the

Grand Canyon of the Colorado and wanting to jump to his death, but being afraid to. The narrator said he went home thinking this was "a mad story," but four days later heard that a young tramp had thrown himself into the Grand Canyon of the Yellowstone. The episode obviously preyed on young Alan's mind. In a poem published seven years later, he recalled or imagined a householder describing a young transient from Brooklyn who had "come, he said, because he'd heard of cliffs / And fathomless canyons in the mountains."[24]

Back home in Powell, Alan rode his motorcycle into town and sold it. He also continued writing poems. As a bright student, he was allowed to skip grades and enter high school early.

Classmate Ross Jamieson recalled that the school was socially divided between the students who lived in town and the "bus kids" who rode in from the country in a Model T bus. "The social activities of the town kids hardly ever included the bus kids," Jamieson said. As the Swallow home was only three miles from town, it was the first stop for the bus, which went about twenty miles picking up other students before reaching the school.

Alan, Jamieson said, "was not anti-social but at the same time he appeared that way . . . he was not popular . . . most of this I think because of his high intellect." A typical report card showed him excelling in English and doing passable work in geometry. Sometimes in class he wrote poetry, paying little or no attention to what the teacher was saying. A girl in the class might get a note from him in the form of a sonnet. His poem "My Ford," combining his interest in poetry and cars, was published

10. The Powell High School building that Alan Swallow attended no longer stands, but officials of the newer school preserved this lintel as a memorial of the place where the future poet and publisher placed second in a graduating class of eight. Photo by Joyce Miller Nelson.

in the school newspaper, the *Powell Powwow*, in January 1932. He also experimented with haiku. By his senior year, he was sending poems to little magazines and getting occasional acceptances.[25]

In September of that year, Alan wrote a poem to a girl named Hazel Peters, saying she was like "the last white rose." By November, he was writing in his diary that he was in love with Hazel. She, however, declined his invitation to a rally, saying she probably would not go, but then showed up at the event with another boy. "He could not make any time with any of the girls in our class," said Jamieson. A group of the more popular girls sometimes tried to get one of them to date Alan, because he had access to the family's late-model sedan, but "had a problem getting one of the bunch to match up" with him. Nevertheless, at five feet ten, 180 pounds, with sandy blonde hair and greenish blue eyes, he was still attractive to some girls.

One night Vera invited her friend Mae Elder out to the house to visit, and Mae discovered that her friend had a brother. That spring another friend invited Mae to go to a club dance with her. Alan was there, she recalled, and "I started dancing with him and we started going together." Mae was a freshman, and Alan was ribbed by his classmates for "robbing the cradle."

The girl's grandparents had come in 1909 from Scranton, Pennsylvania, to Powell, where they bought a previously homesteaded place for $1,967.37. Her parents, Ralph and Isabel Elder, had left Powell when Mae was eight, and she lived with them in various places in Montana, returning just as she was ready to enter high school. She found Alan "a very gentle person" and her parents liked him. The increasingly agnostic youth would argue religion with the Swiss immigrant believer Ralph Elder, keeping Mae waiting to go out dancing.

He wrote poems to Mae at night, with a flashlight, and hid them under his pillow. Vera, whose chores included making the beds, would find the poems and embarrass her brother by reading them to the family. Alan's fun-loving redheaded sister Virginia sometimes showed them to Mae. There began to be talk of marriage. Vera recalled Alan calling a sort of family meeting at which she thought he "still wanted to marry Mae," but wanted his parents to meet "this other girl whom he had met in a literary sort of way." Perhaps this was whom he had in mind in "Golden Girl": someone the narrator met at a dance, was too shy to speak to at first but later became friends with, and then brought her scorn upon him with an unwelcome kiss.

Vera also remembered that Alan, after taking part in a school play, "had a crush on the young English teacher" and may have visited her in her apartment for "intellectual contact." Edgar Swallow preferred Mae for his son, thinking the other girl, whoever she was, had "far reaching ideas about things" that could lead both of them "clear off the deep end." In Powell, said Vera, "mostly they stayed on the farm and married the next door neighbor." Mae was not a next door neighbor; she lived in town. But neither did she meet Alan in any "literary sort of way."[26]

For some reason that nobody among his family or friends seemed to recall, Alan was never called by his name but was known as "Perk." Ross Jamieson thought the nickname was given early, probably before Alan started school. He recalled Edgar Swallow addressing the boy as "Perkins . . . possibly a term of endearment." Vera, who had trouble pronouncing some letters as a child, thought she might have given it to him, as she "had a nickname for most things." Jamieson did not believe it was because Alan was in any way "perky," as he considered him rather aloof. Although the boy was named Edgar after his father, he always used his middle name. In his early writings, he signed himself "E. Alan Swallow."[27]

Edgar Swallow, who was keen on sports but had been too busy as a farmer to spend time on the playing field in his youth, was eager for Alan to go out for football. "He just couldn't imagine a son of his not playing football," Vera said. Alan could imagine it easily, and preferred to be a spectator. In his senior year, however, it was "OK, Dad, I'll go out for football." He did his father proud by making the team but "hated every minute of it," his sister said.[28]

Although he did not become a star on the gridiron, Alan continued to shine in class. He was on the school's debate team for three years and wrote a column in the *Powwow*. In a class of eight graduating seniors, he ranked second. On April 27, 1932, he received an honor scholarship covering all fees at the University of Wyoming. The certificate said he won first place among the boys in his class, as judged by his high school teachers on the basis of his grades, qualities of leadership, and "promise of future usefulness."

The ostensible theme of Alan's salutatorian address at the June commencement exercises was "The Golden Rule," but along the way he reflected on the strengths and shortcomings of education. "For centuries," the seventeen-year-old graduate said, "students have been trained to be blindly patriotic to one nation. Today, the schools teach geographical knowledge of all the nations; a social knowledge of all nationalities; and a historical knowledge

11. As a seventeen-year-old high school salutatorian, Alan Swallow, second from right in the third row, praised schools for encouraging each student "to experiment in a great number of vocations" and not necessarily "follow the business of his father and grandfather." Photo courtesy of Karen Swallow.

of the slow development of the human race from primitive savages, dominated by fear, to civilized people, still dominated, I believe, by fear." However, he said, where in the past it had been customary for a student to follow the business of his father and grandfather, the student now "is encouraged to experiment in a great number of vocations until he finds the one for which he is best suited."[29]

For the trip to the university in Laramie that fall, Alan and his friends Jamieson and Eddie Shawless loaded their goods into a Model T reconstructed into what they called a "bug," a bodiless vehicle much like the racing cars of the day. They had found the parts for it at the Powell city dump, and when the motor blew after they had trouble on some of the hills, they picked up another one from the junk pile in the larger town of Shoshone.[30]

Writing in his notebook before he left, Alan foresaw a university education that would produce "a mind that is practical without being bound by monied [*sic*] and practical interests; a mind with a definite philosophy to guide it through, at best, a life of many troubles and hard knocks." Alan Swallow, publisher, would have his share of those, but he was on his way.[31]

2

Big Man on Campus

Some aspects of the University of Wyoming's "definite philosophy" did not please Alan Swallow after he reached the campus. In an unpublished essay written during his first days at the university, he began, "A student goes to college. He is burning with the desire to study literature, to take journalism and to practice writing. But he is just a freshman—and freshmen aren't allowed to take those courses." ROTC, on the other hand, was required.

By Swallow's account, the commander at the initial class told the students, "If you are a pacifist, you do not belong here . . . You students are too immature to know what you want, to pick out a course, so you need military training. Military training will give you 'guts.'"

After taking an equally dim view of fraternity rush week, where the "condescending collegiates from the old hometown soon snatched him up," Swallow turned to a straw vote in his political science class. Herbert Hoover, the Republican candidate for president, garnered 28 votes, to 26 for his Democratic rival, Franklin D. Roosevelt, and seven for Socialist Norman Thomas.

The narrative went on to say that "the student has one interesting class. It is an informal class in argumentation and debate." One day the unnamed instructor was preparing to give a talk at a teachers' institute, and tried his ideas out on his class. "Most college students," the instructor said, "have little more interest in learning than in knowing the brand of gum they chew." Their graduation, he said, was a joke. "As for the teachers, some are good—but the trouble is the remainder." The instructor then admitted that it wouldn't be practical to say these things to the teachers at the institute, but he was able to get them off his chest in class.[1]

Swallow's other classes as a freshman included chemistry, French, and physical education. He had thought of journalism, but announced his decision to major in English, with minors in sociology and philosophy. He was to win the "President's Book" for outstanding work in all three. Looking back years later, he found life on the Laramie campus "hardly intellectual at all" in a decade "of ferment, of awakened social consciousness, debate over political parties and philosophies."[2]

Despite the onset of the Depression, Laramie, a town founded during the building of the transcontinental railroad in the 1860s, had grown from the 8,609 people counted in the 1930 census to an estimated 11,000 in 1932. The university boasted an enrollment of 1,500 and advertised, "No Where Can You Go to College at Less Cost."[3]

The three freshmen from Powell found a home several blocks from the campus that would take them in for room and board. One night Swallow helped their landlady, laborer's wife Cora Sliger, write a letter of consolation to the husband of a friend who had died. When he came home from school the next day, he heard the radio playing and remembered Mrs. Sliger telling him that she played the radio when she had the "blues" or felt lonely. "It is odd, this feeling of loneliness," he thought. "One feels it so often himself that he awakes with a start when he finds that others feel it too."[4]

One of the roommates would not last long. Ross Jamieson had far outshone Alan Swallow on the Powell football team, and his high school coach thought he was material for the Wyoming Cowboys. His parents did not have the money to send him to the university, but the coach figured he would get "a scholarship or at least some help." Jamieson easily made the university's freshman team, which at that time was used for the varsity to practice against, but received no financial help. He was ready to quit and go home, but Alan loaned him the money to get him through the first quarter. The young Swallow was financially independent enough to write his friend a check for $200 on the Powell bank, apparently without consulting his parents. Jamieson then went home, owing his roommate $200, and went on to a career in business. Alan soon moved also, but only to an apartment closer to the campus.[5]

His political views were already at odds with those of his Republican father. Less than a month after entering the university, he wrote a "very friendly letter" to muckraking California author Upton Sinclair. Judging from Sinclair's reply, the young student asked him to recommend "books which deal with the writer's life, and with literature from the Socialist point of view." Sinclair enclosed a pamphlet and recommended some of his own writing. Later Swallow submitted poems to the left-wing *New Masses* and received a letter from editor Stanley Burnshaw suggesting improvements to make his verse "an adequate, strong, and integral concomitant of proletarian struggle for a new social order—the order based on Marxism and Leninism."[6]

He was home in Powell for Thanksgiving, and wrote a poem to Mae lamenting "those long weary days, / those dead days without you" that he would spend in Laramie.

On his eighteenth birthday, February 11, 1933, he received a box of candy as a present from Mae, asked himself, "Could anyone wish for more?" and answered, "Easily—but it is not good to do so often." The passage is part of an almost daily diary, which he wrote in his Cordiner's Special Composition Book and headed "jottings." He described youth as "a melancholy period" of gazing into the "darkness called 'the future'" and asking, "What does that 'future' hold in store for youth?"[7]

In subsequent jottings he wrote admiringly of Sherwood Anderson, Maxim Gorki, Romain Rolland, Granville Hicks, and others of the "literati leaning left." His reading ranged from the poems of Emily Dickinson to an article on Marxian attitudes toward social organization. Writing of Dickinson, he puzzled over her "strained rhythm" and lack of the "sameness of meter that carries the tongue along." He found critic Burton Rascoe intriguing, but chided him for making "no reference to the new, ascendant, radical literature except only to list the name of John Dos Passos." He deplored "the creeping of sex into biography" in lives of Shelley, Byron, and others, arguing that "certainly little mention of an Oedipus complex or homosexuality would be necessary" in writing of the life of Emerson, Thoreau, or even Whitman.

He read A. E. Housman because defense lawyer Clarence Darrow had admired and quoted him. In the English poet he detected comfort "for the Agnostic and the Free Thinker who does not dull his mind with the opiates of religion and vain hopes."[8]

It was probably in this year that he began serving as volunteer manager for a local baseball team during the summer, prefiguring a lifelong fondness for the game.

By October, though, it was back to literature. An unofficial literary magazine, *Sage,* appeared on the campus at five cents a copy, with Alan as editor and Madolin Shorey and Bill Pedigo as associate editors. The magazine was mimeographed, and even thirty-three years later, Alan Swallow would reflect that "undoubtedly the mimeograph will be an honored machine." The initial issue announced a "Dedication to a more active interest in literature on the campus of the University of Wyoming." A lead editorial proclaimed that "new approaches, new methods, new values" had become apparent since the onset of the Depression. "It is the purpose of the editors of *Sage* to provide a medium of expression for those interested in this most modern literature," the neophyte editor wrote. "Any type of opinion will be allowed as long as it concerns modern American literature and is substantiated by arguments. And since this is a period of revaluation in all kinds and forms of individual and social thinking, *Sage* will take part in the asking and answering of the question, 'Whither the American writer?'" The magazine carried poetry by Swallow and other student poets, as well as fiction. Its title was in part a reference to Wyoming vegetation and in part a pun on the supposed wisdom of its editors.[9]

Sometime early in his sophomore year, Alan conceived the idea of cutting loose from the university and trying his fortunes in New York. In a fatherly "Dear Perk" letter, Edgar Swallow urged his only son to "go on to school there in Laramie until you finish your four years of college, at least go the rest of this school year. You have the opportunity now and if you quit you may never have the chance again . . . If you can just keep your feet on the ground for a year or two yet I believe that you will get over this restlessness." He cautioned Alan that he was unlikely to get work in New York during the deepening Depression, advising him that "there are several million men looking for these jobs all the time." The letter was signed "With love, Dad."

Edgar had given up farming because of heart trouble and moved into Powell, turning a farm laborer's house into a home for his mother, Ida. His letter to Alan was written on the letterhead of Bloom & Swallow, Implements, Coal, Produce, Powell, Wyo. Business was "awfully quiet," he said. "Seems impossible to make any collections." He feared he might have to go back to the farm. In a poem "For My Father" at about this time, the son wrote, "What does it matter that the back curved / Finally? A work is done, an epoch / Finished rightly."[10]

The fatherly advice prevailed, and Alan concentrated much of his energy on his first publishing venture, *Sage*. The first issue had been tentative, to test the waters. "The idea was to start with local talent, in the hope that gradually the magazine could extend beyond the campus to reach for additional talent and more mature talent and also for reading response," the young editor said. By December he and his colleagues had decided there was enough interest to continue publication. English professor V. C. Coulter had declared the magazine worthwhile. Pedigo had been dropped from the masthead, and Shorey's position renamed assistant editor. She was a good typist, and her duties included preparing the stencils used in the mimeographing process. She also criticized her editor's poems, saying a sonnet about Hart Crane was "rather obscure." Alan sent the poem to Laramie poet Ted Olson, a winner in the Yale Series of Younger Poets competition, and Olson agreed with Shorey, saying, "Perhaps obscurity is justified in a sonnet on Crane, but I think you can make your meaning a little more lucid."[11]

At Christmas of his sophomore year, Alan drove home with "a carload of kids" to visit his family and Mae. Taking an unfamiliar and hilly two-lane highway, he collided with another car, perhaps driven drunkenly. Swallow called home in the middle of the night for his father to come and get them. Nobody was seriously hurt, but when Edgar Swallow saw the wreckage with baggage strewn around it, "he didn't see how anybody could have survived."[12]

At a meeting with some high school classmates, Swallow urged one of them to contribute to *Sage,* but she declined on grounds that she lacked literary ability and that her "present status, mental and otherwise, is entirely too erratic (not erotic) to write intelligently." She told him that his should be a literary career but that "your little town has crushed me, irretrievably."[13]

The January issue featured a review of the novel *In Tragic Life,* by Vardis Fisher, who would become one of Alan's closest friends and sternest critics. The Idaho writer was praised for a "piling up of incident after incident and scene after scene that mark the profound influence upon a sensitive child of a Northwest environment, an environment still frontier-like in many of its aspects." The word *environment* was used, as was common at the time, to refer to home influences rather than those of nature and the outdoors. In a bylined review, Swallow took on the "tumultuous visionings" of Hart Crane's *The Bridge,* the "mystical knowledge that sees life as life and not as something with which to grasp money." He found Crane one of the most interesting of "the group of modern writers who have tried . . . to tie the past with the present and both of these into the future."[14]

Shorey was editor of the February issue and presumably responsible for an editorial saying the editors had on the one hand "heard the magazine praised for its general excellence, and on the other . . . heard it condemned as rotten." On the whole, the editorial said, "compared to the usual college literary magazine, we feel that we need not be ashamed." The journal had grown from its initial twelve pages to eighteen and contained a Swallow poem showing that the young author had fallen prey to the blues. It was snowing, he wrote, and "I should like to run madly through the soft, clinging snow, / But I can't. I can only sit here, crying."

Swallow was back as editor for the last issue of the first academic year, conceding that *Sage* had "not published any great literature" and had run into financial problems, but adding that "above all, we have stirred up a little interest in writing." In the end, he concluded that the course he had followed was in most cases "not a sound idea for launching a magazine." He "resolved that at some time I would be back into publishing a magazine" but "less with a local situation and to be able to publish more mature writers whom I admired."[15]

Alan began assembling what he entitled *A New Poetry* with the subheading "An Anthology Compiled by Alan Swallow." The published work, beginning with the English poets W. H. Auden and C. Day Lewis, was clipped from magazines. He was still collecting the clippings as late as 1937, the year of his graduation, when he clipped Richard Eberhart's "If I could live at the pitch that is near madness" from the left-wing *New Masses*.[16]

Mae Elder's parents, meanwhile, had sent her to Billings, Montana, to attend business school. Mae recalled later that "we were supposed to be separated to see what we were eventually going to do" and that "we thought this was a good idea, we were young." Perhaps also her parents thought that if she were going to marry Alan Swallow, it would be good to have somebody in the family with a head for business.[17]

Mae was back in Powell when Alan returned in the summer of 1936 to take a year off from higher education after his junior year and try to decide what his future was to be. Other students, notably the future Wyoming poet laureate Peggy Simpson Curry, tried to continue *Sage,* but it petered out. The magazine was reincarnated in the 1960s as a University of Wyoming humanities review far different from "the youthful, not-dry-behind-the-ears" effort of the 1930s.

In Powell Alan alternated working in the fields and as bookkeeper and teller in a bank. Vera thought that maybe he came back to make money so that Mae could go to

12. In June 1936 Alan Swallow and Mae Elder of Powell were married. They posed for this picture while on an outing to a rocky area near the university. Despite marital troubles, she would be with him until his death. Photo courtesy of Karen Swallow.

Laramie with him. They were married in June 1936. He was twenty-one and she eighteen.

His love for his bride was mingled with his love of powered vehicles, and that passion now pushed him to aerial pursuits. He owned, he said, a part interest in three airplanes. For one of them, a two-wing, two-seat craft, he hired a pilot from Billings to teach him to fly, paying him by allowing him to use the plane to make money barnstorming at county fairs. Mae went along on some of these learning flights, edgy at first because the pilot seemed to her to have had a few beers beforehand. Vera remembered the fun of "riding in the plane, and the pilot turning loops in the air." Before Alan learned to solo, the pilot took the plane to the Wyoming State Fair in Douglas and crashed it while stunting. The plane was not insured, and the aviation era ended. In a poem Alan wrote that his ventures into the "brittle steeps of air" were "clean as steel / and breathless as a song."[18]

For his senior year, he and Mae found an apartment nearer to downtown Laramie than to the campus.[19] Mae enrolled as a student. Her husband became news editor of the student newspaper, *The Branding Iron,* and continued active in debate. At the annual Rocky Mountain speech conference for teachers, students, and speakers, he and fellow student Clifford Hansen argued against the proposition "that the powers of the president should be substantially increased as a matter of settled policy." President Franklin D. Roosevelt had assumed emergency powers to deal with the Depression, but Swallow and Hansen argued that the danger of making these powers permanent would be too great. Hansen later entered politics as a Republican and served Wyoming as governor and then as a U.S. senator during the era when his party was defending Richard Nixon's expansive view of presidential power. The conference was held at the University of Denver, where Alan would spend not always happy years as a teacher and editor.[20]

For the present, he was elected to membership, on the basis of a manuscript he submitted, in the Wyoming chapter of the American College Quill Club. After paying a $10 initiation fee, he served on a committee to select manuscripts for publication in the spring issue of the club's journal, *Wyoming Quill.*[21] Two other clubs, the Cosmopolitan and the poetry group Skalds, elected him vice president.[22] He won the $10 first prize in the school's A. C. Jones poetry competition for a poem called "Weed-Smoke" in which he recalled "the lighting of a dry crushed tumble-weed, / And the quick leap of flame up into gray smoke in the wind." In a small way he was becoming something of a big man on campus.[23]

Alan Swallow's name was appearing more and more often over poems in the proliferating "little magazines." In his freshman year he was published as E. Alan Swallow. As a sophomore he dropped the initial, although he wrote a sequence of three sonnets to Hart Crane under his full name, Edgar Alan Swallow. Wilson Clough, a professor of American Studies at the university, took an interest in his work and prided himself on "observing the signs that his would be something more than the usual brief flirtation with the medium of verse."[24]

One of his first published poems was a Shakespearean sonnet, "To Men I Have Known," that appeared in the July 1934 *Kaleidograph*. It showed the influences both of his reading in nineteenth-century poetry and of his growing up on the Powell Flat:

> Who will lament these sons of soil who plod
> So wearily homeward in the shadowed dusk?
> When these hard forms are laid beside a clod,
> Who—standing in another echoed dusk—
> Who will remember all these patient days
> Of bending over small bewildered blades,
> Of wresting life from cold, unfeeling clays
> In work so kind and yet whose memory fades?
>
> These weary forms have yet no monument.
> They do not wish someone to mourn for them.

> Their thoughts are of the hours of toil well spent
> As homeward to their peaceful requiem
> Of sleep they slowly plod. But ages hence
> Who will recall they passed along this fence?

The April 1937 *College Verse* included a group of Swallow poems, including two sonnets to Mae and a tightly written piece on "Wyoming's January" that showed unease with the Wyoming climate and foreshadowed his more mature work:

> I am afraid of spring,
> Afraid that vagrant snow
> Will, melting, never bring
> The things that grow.
>
> For here the sterile breast
> Of earth is always bare
> But for the hawk at rest
> Sitting the air.
>
> And now that I can see
> The veil that winters bring,
> The eyes are cowardly,
> Afraid of spring.

Alan was instrumental in inviting Monroe Sweetland, a member of the Student League for Industrial Democracy, to the campus to seek creation of a local chapter. The following week Alan was elected president of the chapter, with Clifford Hansen as vice president. The group was represented on about two hundred college campuses and published a monthly magazine, *The Student Outlook*.

The national organization's membership included the perennial Socialist Party presidential candidate Norman Thomas, educator John Dewey, writer Stuart Chase, and journalist Joseph P. Lash. Speaking at a weekly lecture series sponsored by the chapter, Alan declared that American literature was moving "from marked individualism to a social consciousness" as manifested by "a sympathy toward communism on the part of a large number of our important authors." He said small-circulation literary magazines were "leaving off the old themes of sex" and "writing with a definite social philosophy in mind."[25]

Alan also returned to the subject of military training. In a guest editorial in *The Branding Iron,* he wound up with this rousing peroration about what he called the military formula:

> It's making the world safe that matters. It's the
>   formula that
> Matters. Learn it. Remember it. It's one, two, three,
>   four, plus
> Heil, Hitler! Heil!

The young poet obtained the signatures of forty-one students to a statement opposing compulsory military education. The statement took issue with a radio address on the subject that the president of the university, Arthur G. Crane, had made at a national conference. Swallow and Hansen issued an open challenge to a debate on the issue. Their debate resolution read, "Resolved, that a protest against military training is fully justified by the unlikelihood of the United States' engaging in a genuinely defensive war." Within a decade, after the Japanese

13. At the University of Wyoming, Alan Swallow challenged the school's president, Arthur G. Crane, shown in this portrait, to a debate after Crane spoke in support of compulsory ROTC at a national conference. Photo courtesy of the American Heritage Center, University of Wyoming.

attack on Pearl Harbor, Alan Swallow would be in an army uniform.[26]

Alan was by no means alone in his anti–ROTC sentiments. An official army history of the corps said it faced controversy from its inception in 1916 and later confronted "an inhospitable collegiate environment—caused in part by the pacifist sentiment that became prevalent in the American college community after World War I." Alan's efforts were unsuccessful, and compulsory ROTC was not abolished at the university until the middle 1960s, when the program was under assault by opponents of the U.S. role in the Vietnam War. Other land-grant institutions made the program optional at about the same time, and nine universities discontinued it altogether.[27]

At 10 AM on June 8, 1937, a Tuesday, Swallow joined other graduating seniors in University Auditorium to

14. At University of Wyoming commencement on June 8, 1937, Alan Swallow, far left in the back row, was one of eight students, out of a class of 169, to receive the bachelor of arts degree with honor. Photo courtesy of Karen Swallow.

receive his bachelor of arts at a ceremony opening with Wagner's "Tannhauser March." He was one of eight students, out of a class of 169, to receive the Bachelor of Arts degree with honor. The commencement speech on "The University's Service to Wyoming" was delivered by Frank Pierrepont Graves, who had been the university's president from 1896 to 1898.[28]

What to do next? Alan, "still not clear on how to make a go of things with my interest in writing," was considering an offer to be editor of a small weekly newspaper. There was also talk of going back to the farm and living in a small house formerly occupied by a hired man who had moved into the larger family home when Alan's parents moved to town. Vera Swallow, however, did not think Alan Swallow would ever be a farmer.[29]

Shortly before graduation, a letter arrived from Louisiana State University that opened new possibilities. The judges of a competition sponsored by the magazine *College Verse* announced the annual Virginia awards to the most promising poets they had published during the year. The judges were Robert Penn Warren, a young assistant professor of English at Louisiana State University, later to win the Pulitzer Prize three times and become his country's first official poet laureate; John Crowe Ransom, professor of English at Vanderbilt University, to be a winner of the Bollingen Prize for poetry; and Robert P. Tristram Coffin of Wells University, New York. They awarded the first prize to Clark Mills of Washington University, and gave Alan Swallow of the University of Wyoming and Valvia Boston of Tennessee Teachers College honorable mention. Warren said, "I feel that Clark Mills and Alan Swallow are decisively ahead of the field." He thought Swallow's work showed "more lapses than that of Clark Mills," but also demonstrated "positive attempts, often successful, to solve them."[30]

The die was cast. "Powell," Alan Swallow's daughter was to say years later, "was nowhere to stay."[31]

3

Down Altitudes of Air

I n a collection of essays, *I'll Take My Stand,* published in 1930, Robert Penn Warren and eleven other young writers embraced to varying degrees the heritage of the Confederacy and denounced with equal fervor both American industrialism and Soviet communism. They marched under the banner of the Southern Agrarians, although one poet and critic who was also a part-time farmer derided them as agrarians who knew nothing about farming. The title of their book was derived from the Daniel Emmett song "Dixie," with the refrain "In Dixie's Land, we'll took our stand, / To lib an' dic in Dixie." (Emmett, writing for popular minstrel shows in which white men wore makeup to darken their faces, emulated incorrect grammar assumed to be characteristic of black slaves in the South.) Warren's essay was entitled "The Briar Patch," a phrase from Joel Chandler Harris's condescending Uncle Remus stories. Warren had chosen, he said, to write "the essay on the negro."

The racial implications of both the titles and the works that appeared beneath them understandably stirred controversy throughout the 1930s and beyond. In Warren's essay, he postulated a situation in which an African American man was turned away from a whites-only hotel, and

15. As a young assistant professor of
English at Louisiana State University, the future Pulitzer Prize winner Robert Penn Warren awarded
Alan Swallow honorable mention in
a national poetry contest, declaring
him "decisively ahead of the field."
In this 1937 photo, Warren is at
the left with T. S. Stribling outside
an LSU building where the visiting
writer addressed students. Charles
East Papers, Mss. 3471, Louisiana and
Lower Mississippi Valley Collections,
LSU Libraries, Baton Rouge, LA.

asked, "Does he simply want to spend the night in a hotel as comfortable as one from which he is turned away, or does he want to spend the night in that same hotel? A good deal depends on how this hypothetical negro would answer the question." Warren, born and raised in the southern Kentucky town of Guthrie, clearly answered it in favor of the "separate but equal" doctrine that was then the law of the land.[1]

Other essays in the book dealt with economics, agriculture, the arts, education, philosophy, and religion from what the authors saw as the southern perspective. The literary critic and folklorist Donald Davidson wrote that the ascendancy of industrialism "will mean that there will be no arts left to foster; or, if they exist at all, they will flourish only in a diseased and disordered condition." John Crowe Ransom attacked "the gospel of Progress," which he said "never defines its ultimate objective." His fellow poet Allen Tate, a recent convert to the Roman Catholic faith, said the religion of America was "a religion of the half horse . . . preeminently a religion of how things work."

The group started a magazine, called *The Fugitive*. In its initial issue in April 1922, Ransom said that the magazine "flees from nothing faster than from the high-caste Brahmins of the Old South." Nevertheless the agrarian doctrine that presumably bound them together was perhaps most forthrightly stated by Andrew Nelson Lytle, a member of a leading family in Murfreesboro, Tennessee, who had been a fellow student with Warren at Vanderbilt University. Lytle urged the farmer to reject well-meaning assurances of "how great is his deserving" and "keep to his ancient ways and leave the homilies of the tumble-bellied prophets to the city man who understands such things." It is an understandable and defensible argument, and according to it Alan Swallow would have stayed on the farm.[2]

He did not. As editor of *Sage,* Swallow had met Gardner Kirk, a paper salesman who was in and out of University of Wyoming offices. Kirk was now studying at Louisiana State University, and wrote his Laramie acquaintance assuring him that he could get a fellowship for graduate study at the Louisiana school. There would be no farming or journalism for Alan Swallow. He and Mae were off for Baton Rouge, with a stop in Gerard, Kansas, so that Alan could see the Haldeman-Julius publishing plant, source of the Little Blue Books that had so fired his imagination at a Montana filling station. Inside, he looked around and found a box of Haldeman-Julius books for a dollar each. As they drove on toward Louisiana, Mae took each one out of the box and read the title. If Alan did not have it, they kept it. If he did, they "threw it out the window for some farmer to pick up and read."[3]

Alan reflected on the transition from Powell and Laramie to Baton Rouge in a poem, "Road South: Wyoming to Louisiana," writing, "To travel South is not to take / A road, but rapid skier's slide: / Down altitudes of air we break / To land that opens level, wide." After four years in windy southeastern Wyoming, he also found himself in a land where "no wind ever drives the days." He said he and Mae were dismayed to find how "very little change" there was between the southern winter and the southern spring.[4]

The young couple was also confronted with changes that might have been more daunting than the differences between the high plains of Wyoming and the moss-hung live oaks of Louisiana. In the years to come, most of the *I'll Take My Stand* writers drifted away, not only from the South, but from agrarianism. The poet Ransom moved to Iowa, Allen Tate to Minnesota, Warren to Connecticut. Critic Davidson remained a segregationist to the end, but Warren was already altering his views on racial integration when the Supreme Court swept away "separate but equal" with its decision in the *Brown v. Board of Education* school desegregation case in 1954.

When young Alan Swallow rolled into Baton Rouge, however, Warren's support for the rights of black Americans was gradualist to say the most, and the agrarians were still in the saddle. The would-be contributor to *New Masses* found himself surrounded by conservatives with views alien to his. Mae said that Robert Penn Warren and his colleague Cleanth Brooks "wanted him to become, I am sure, a Southern Agrarian," but without success. Alan Swallow was outraged by the treatment of black people that he saw. Later he would cool to the literary works of the agrarians, calling in a 1959 article for "some sound sifting" of their doctrines and arguing that "the cult of Faulkner . . . is dying gradually, and properly so . . . because he is not worth so much as all that."[5]

In addition to all these concerns, the military traditions of LSU were alien to the entrenched foe of compulsory military training. In the institution's early days, military training was not only compulsory, it was a main reason for the school's existence. When it was founded in

1860, it was called The Louisiana Seminary of Learning and Military Academy. Its superintendent was William Tecumseh Sherman, soon to opt for the Union side in the Civil War that destroyed the academy at about the same time General Sherman was leading his destructive march through Georgia and South Carolina.

The college, known familiarly as "The Old War Skule," was rebuilt after the war, but struggled for existence until the emergence of Louisiana's demagogic Governor Huey Long in the 1930s. The colorful governor funneled millions into his vision of making LSU one of the nation's outstanding universities. Warren and other rising young poets and critics were wooed away from Vanderbilt University in Tennessee, and others came from elsewhere.[6]

Mae said the Swallows came to Baton Rouge with no assurance that Alan would really get a fellowship. However, Warren soon prevailed on Graduate School Dean Charles Wooten Pipkin to grant the young man from Wyoming a reading fellowship, grading papers, for his first year. The position carried a small stipend in addition to the free tuition that was part of Governor Long's largesse. Pipkin also lined Mae up with a secretarial job at the *Southern Review*. Two years earlier, he, Warren, and Brooks had been granted $10,000 a year by the university to publish the review, which would become one of the most distinguished literary journals in the English language. The *Review* was discontinued in 1942 under the pressures of World War II and revived in 1965.[7]

Mae Swallow was a resilient young woman. Her family had left Powell after she completed the second grade and moved to Montana, where her father, a mechanic, worked successively in Hobson, Great Falls, and Billings. They did not return to Powell until the summer before she entered high school and met Alan. She enjoyed traveling with her husband, and as for settling down in Powell, she said, "Oh, no. No. I liked Powell; it was OK but I had so many relatives they were always behind every tree so they kept track of every move you made."

After graduation, she had enjoyed her year at business school in Billings, at least part of the time. She liked the bookkeeping, which she used later in life, but hated taking dictation in shorthand. She had to do shorthand in her job at the *Southern Review,* but said she "got by on the dictation somehow or other after the first letter or two." She also found it exciting: "all the correspondence you can imagine came and went from that office." Other duties included correcting proof, folding and gathering pages, and wrapping magazines to be mailed (poet Robert Lowell later tried to help with the wrapping, but was said to be "not terribly handy" at it).

Mae had taken over from an experienced secretary and felt shaky in the job, but found business manager Albert Erskine and his associates forgiving about being served by somebody who was "still just a kid." Brooks said they found her excellent. "They didn't bother us," she said. Erskine, in fact, spent a good deal of time in a room across the hall playing chess. The writer Jean Stafford, who followed Mae as secretary to the review, said that Erskine and Brooks were "nice to work for" although the office "looks like a hog sty with an accumulation of years of manuscript."

Mae was the journal's only full-time employee; Erskine, an LSU graduate student, was quarter time, as were the three editors—Warren, Brooks, and Pipkin—who were given reduced teaching loads. It must have been a lively place to work, with the editors arguing about contributions from authors who ranged from college sophomores to Nobel Prize winners. Swallow later wrote that the magazine's willingness to embrace "a point of view which would cover all" led to the selection of "good materials from people who were not Southern Agrarians." Mae liked her job, but had no interest in going into literary publishing herself, and saw no signs that her husband was being groomed for the field.[8]

At home, one of her domestic chores was to make roll-your-own cigarettes on a manual device. The apartment they had found was upstairs over the landlord, and the humid heat of Baton Rouge was torment for a young couple accustomed to the dry climate of the Rockies. When Alan came down with a cold in August, they tried the remedy they had used at home: a sweat bath that sent the patient to bed perspiring. When the landlady said she had never heard of such a thing as a sweat bath, they tried riding a ferry back and forth across the Mississippi River to cool off. "It's a wonder we didn't kill him but he came out of it OK," Mae said. "Never did that again."[9]

Whatever Mae thought, immersion in this Deep South atmosphere was taking her young husband aback. During his first summer at Baton Rouge, Alan asked a correspondent in Missoula, Montana, about possibly opening a bookstore in that city. "Missoula is not a book buying community," he was told. "I would not wish to encourage you strongly to venture into the book business here."[10] Studying Romantic poets with Brooks and Warren, Swallow

16. The newcomers from Wyoming tried riding a ferry back and forth across the Mississippi River to fight the Louisiana heat. Photo courtesy of Karen Swallow.

was finding graduate study at LSU tougher than his undergraduate days in Laramie. Over his three academic years at LSU, he made A in most of his courses, but B in Restoration Drama, Old English, and Beowulf.[11] Sometimes, Mae said, "he didn't really know a lot what they were talking about. So he had lots of studying to do."

In addition, he found Warren's southern Kentucky accent and staccato style of speaking difficult to understand.[12] "In the first class I had with him, it was six weeks before I was sure I knew what he was saying," Alan said.[13] To compensate, Robert Penn Warren had a notably warm and kind manner with not only hard-working master's degree candidates but even freshmen struggling with English composition.[14] Alan found some of the attitudes toward poetry shown by Warren and others at LSU, perhaps Warren's emphasis on "the tension between the rhythm of the poem and the rhythm of speech," unsound.[15] As he said looking back from the vantage point of the 1950s, "I knew it at the time, but not so well as I knew it considerably later when I found some of the attitudes hard to shrug off."[16]

Brooks recalled Alan as "a first-rate student," but did not recognize his talents until after he had left the university. He saw a great deal of him, he said, although he misspelled his first name.[17]

An activist as he had been at the University of Wyoming, Alan organized an LSU chapter of the Poetry Society of America after corresponding with the group's executive secretary, Ann Winslow. He had known her as a professor at the University of Wyoming. He was also busy submitting poetry and prose to magazines. *The Intermountain Review* of Cedar City, Utah, accepted an article on Robinson Jeffers but returned essays on William Butler Yeats and "Four Ways of Modern Man" on grounds that, like his poems in Laramie, they were obscure. For relaxation, the young couple found time for a visit to New Orleans. Before leaving, they sought advice from a "broken down aristocrat," who had sent Alan poems, on how to find inexpensive places to visit in the French Quarter.[18]

For their first Louisiana Christmas, the Swallows sent friends an irreverent greeting featuring a ballad by Alan about a monk who falls from a slippery log and drowns in a moat while on his way to an assignation with a young woman. Angels and devils battle for his soul, the angels arguing that the monk had not as yet done anything sinful. The adversaries submit the case to the king, who decrees that the monk should be given another chance. The nar-

rative concludes: "This time with surer step, he crossed /
The water, and went in."[19]

Midway in his first year at LSU, Swallow became Louisiana editor of *The North America Book of Verse,* an anthology being founded by the decade-old New York–based
monthly magazine *Poetry World.* There was no pay, but he
was promised reimbursement for any of the postage-due
envelopes that editor Daniel Harrison predicted he would
receive. He had to keep 3x5 file cards for records of the
names and addresses of Louisiana poets submitting work,
whether accepted or not. At the end of the academic year,
he had the assignment of writing a foreword to the Louisiana section of the anthology.[20]

His reading fellowship expired at the end of the year,
and he received a teaching fellowship for the next two
years. That summer he and Mae returned to Powell, taking an LSU student, Louis Morrow, home with them.
By January 1939, Swallow was telling Ted Olson that the
"academic drudgery" of his new fellowship was the worst
so far. Nevertheless he continued writing poems and sending them for criticism to Olson, now in New York and
writing for the *Herald-Tribune* after eleven years with the
Laramie Republican-Boomerang. Olson found Alan's "command of phrase and rhythm becoming more shrewd and
accurate" and recommended that he think about submitting a collection for the Yale Series. While he was writing poetry in the mid-twentieth-century mode, Swallow
immersed himself in scholarly study of the cultural values
of the sixteenth and seventeenth.[21]

Always a follower of the news, Alan may well have
encountered in a Baton Rouge newspaper the name of

a would-be bank robber named Earl Durand. Durand was big news throughout the country, and brought newsreel cameras and *Life* magazine photographers to Powell, Wyoming. Although Alan probably did not immediately know it, his bank vice president father was a supporting player in the Durand melodrama.

To a country in the grip of the Depression, real-life gangster epics were often a welcome touch of the romantic. In the classic 1939 John Ford movie *Stagecoach,* the outlaw Ringo, played by John Wayne, is the hero, and the town banker is an embezzler. There was nothing very romantic, however, about Durand. Like Alan Swallow, he was a farm boy. Unlike Alan, he had a reputation for not being "what you might call completely civilized." Part of each year, he lived in a sheep wagon or a tent outside his parents' house. He quit school early and for a while drove a school bus, quite likely the one the Swallow kids rode on. He disdained farm work and would be gone for weeks at a time, taking long hikes around the Flat and up into the mountains. He liked raw meat and liked to hunt, paying little attention to the game laws or, as it turned out, to any laws. Powell had spawned a figure who would be as unlikely a contrast with its small-town calm as the brilliant literary Alan Swallow.

On March 13, 1939, Durand talked farmer Emil Knopp, the farmer's sixteen-year-old son Ronnie, and a neighbor boy into poaching elk with him. The boys were caught, but Durand slipped away, leaving his companions to face the music. The next day a posse caught him and he was sentenced to sixty days in the Park County jail in Cody. Two days later, he escaped and killed two law officers who went after him. One of them, town marshal Charles Lewis, was a Powell native who had returned home after service with the National Guard pursuing the Mexican revolutionary leader Pancho Villa along the U.S.-Mexico border.

As the search for Durand intensified, the outlaw killed two vigilantes who had tagged along with a formal posse convened by the county sheriff. Durand left his mountain hideout, gathered guns and ammunition from reluctant neighbors, hitched a ride from an unwitting radio operator, and descended on Powell's First National Bank. As the outlaw ran into the bank at 1:30 PM with a satchel full of rattling shells, Edgar Swallow was waiting on Vastalee Dutton and her mother. The elder woman had just endorsed a check and slipped it through the brass grill when Durand fired.

Everyone commented on how bomb-like the shot sounded in the marble cavern characteristic of 1930s banks. Edgar Swallow's face turned white as Durand's shots skimmed overhead. The gunman shot out the bank's high windows and ordered the four employees and five customers to line up against a wall, their hands in the air. He forced a bank officer to open a vault and hand over $2,000, but he still seemed to want more. Suddenly he called for some of the men to come and join him where he stood. Edgar, standing next to Vastalee Dutton, stepped forward, but Durand apparently recognized him as a prominent figure in the community. (Alan's Republican father had run unsuccessfully for the legislature in the Roosevelt landslide year of 1936, served a term as mayor, and continued to agitate against one-crop farming.) Durand told him to go back to his place by the wall. Then the ruffian tied three men to a teller's cage, one of them with a lace he had lifted from the boot of one of his victims.

The shooting in the bank attracted fire from townspeople who had come downtown armed. There was so much firing it was hard to determine the source of a shot, but one of the three tied men, twenty-one-year-old bank employee Johnny Gawthrop, was shot and died of his wound. Another shot, fired by a Powell teenager who had come downtown to kill time, felled Durand as he stepped onto the sidewalk. The would-be robber crawled back into the bank, pulled out a six-shooter, and took his own life with a shot to the neck.

Edgar Swallow went back to work and deposited the check written by Vastalee's mother.[22]

Back in Louisiana, Edgar Swallow's son had completed his master's degree in one year, writing his thesis on "The Method of Composition in the Poems of Sir Thomas Wyatt," the sixteenth-century English courtier and poet whose rhythmic patterns have puzzled scholars and won praise from critics and readers. He applied to the University of California for doctoral study under Willard Farnham, who had been a student of Warren's. Farnham's former mentor gave the Wyoming youth a warm recommendation, saying, "He strikes me as a first-rate man. His reading has been wide; his development this year has been unusually rapid; he has a good philosophical and critical bent." Nevertheless, the officials in Berkeley turned him down.[23]

As he pursued a PhD in the 1939–40 school year at LSU, Alan's thoughts turned to publishing and he found that "possibly the opportunity had come for which I had been looking."[24] Like him, a number of promising young writers on the campus had been appearing in the little magazines. Two of them, Sheila Corley and Frederick Brantley, proposed an anthology of writings by some of the students who had been working with Warren and Brooks.[25] The two LSU colleagues were already teaching the principles that would guide their classic textbooks *Understanding Poetry* and *Understanding Fiction*. The idea behind the books, as Brooks explained it, was that although LSU students were bright, "the textbooks that we were dealt out to teach them with were no help at all," concentrating as they did on dates, information about the author, and notes explaining literary allusions. "Suppose," said Brooks, "the boy or girl, however bright, has never had anybody talk to them about how a poem is constructed or what the makeup of a short story is or what kind of truth it conveys . . . we had to try to devise our own textbooks to answer that problem."[26]

In the fall of 1939, Swallow borrowed $100 from his banker father and bought a used five-by-eight Kelsey handpress, with a type case two-thirds regular size. He read as many books as he could find in the LSU library's excellent collection of works on the history of type, printing, and typography. After setting up the press in the garage of the apartment where he and Mae were living, he set to work on *Signets: An Anthology of Beginnings*. The book, one scholar has observed, was "by no means one of the forgotten treasures of American literature," but it sold enough copies to enable him to repay his father's loan. It was also a beginning for the publisher as well as the writers, the first appearance of the imprint "Alan Swallow, Publisher."

With his small handpress, Alan could only set and print one page before breaking up the frame of type. This limited him to doing one page per day. He balked at redistributing the type to the cases, and had students come day after day to handle the tedious chore.

The collection contained two poems by Alan that Olson had liked "immensely." In one of them, entitled simply "Poem," he recalled a love encounter under a long-stemmed pine and said, "This crumbling, spun-out world is yours and mine." The other, a less sanguine piece called "Landscape," cast a cold eye on a land in which "Magnolias weight the air with bloom. The oak, / Gathering green leaves and faded moss, has need / Of rot. The leaf's green flesh is high within / The vulture's tent, and where the vultures feed."

One day early in 1940, Brantley brought Alan a sheaf of manuscripts by a new graduate student poet on the campus, Thomas McGrath. Reading them through as he sat against the wall of the garage, Alan felt "great elation and a great shock." Seeking out McGrath for a meeting, he resolved that his second publishing venture would be a small collection of the newcomer's poems. It would be the beginning of a long relationship between the publisher and the poet, who quickly found themselves congenial. Both were born on western farms, McGrath in North Dakota, and both were holding up the political left in a nest of conservatives. Reflecting later on these early days in his publishing career, Alan believed that his homestead background had given him a tendency "to act upon one's beliefs and ideas . . . the innate character trait toward action."

The anthology appeared in March 1940, and McGrath's *First Manifesto* shortly afterward. The *Manifesto* was the first of a series of Swallow Pamphlets and was priced at twenty-five cents in deference to "the notion, gained from reading the Haldeman-Julius materials, that good literature ought to be put out at a very inexpensive price." Alan Swallow, it was clear, would be a publisher. Looking at the first two publications, he "knew I could put on paper in a workmanlike fashion some of the things I would be wanting to publish."[27]

Alan asked Warren to recommend a worthy poet unpublished in book form. Warren suggested Lincoln Fitzell, a "tall, blond and completely naïve" young man he had roomed with as a graduate student in Berkeley. The budding publisher had seen and admired Fitzell's work in *The Southern Review,* and wrote to him inviting a submission. Fitzell answered that he would like very much to be published by Swallow, but not as a pamphlet. He enclosed a full-length manuscript, *In Plato's Garden,* for which Alan offered a print run of six hundred copies of a ninety-page clothbound book. The royalty offered was 10 percent of gross receipts on the first two hundred copies, and 15 percent on all others, to be paid twice yearly.[28]

Alan's plan was to do his own printing, saving the expense of hiring a printer and enabling him to pay his authors a royalty. His type was getting worn out, however. William Kendall, an LSU political scientist, put him in touch with a Chicago typographer who advised him on selection of typefaces. By chance, the typographer was doing the layout for the magazine *Modern Verse,* of which Alan Swallow would become publisher.

One of the poets Alan invited to submit manuscripts, Raymond Dannenbaum, earned his living working for Twentieth Century–Fox Film Corporation. Dannenbaum did not have a collection ready at the time, but said he was interested and admired Swallow's audacious publishing plan, "although books, pamphlets and a magazine seem almost too much to be done on one hand press."[29]

By this time, Alan was already looking for a job teaching, which would be his main occupation for the next fourteen years. Olson, Brooks, and others wrote recommendations to the University of New Mexico. Alan had indicated he would carry on his publishing while at UNM, and T. M. Pearce, acting head of the English Department there, welcomed the idea. Alan had feelers out at a couple of other universities also, and Warren put in a word for him at Bennington College in Vermont. Still, there were no firm commitments. He thought he could get a teaching fellowship at LSU for another year, but he was not enthusiastic about teaching there. "Were it not for you and Mr. Brooks," he wrote Warren, "the graduate work in English here would not be anything to walk across the street about." With the increasing emphasis on traditional approaches to literature, as opposed to those championed by Brooks and Warren, he had concluded that "there is no place, even temporarily, for me as a teacher here."[30]

He had finished course work for his doctorate and was working with Warren on his dissertation on "the methods of composition which were developed by the poets of the early Renaissance." It was not until June 2, 1941, at the eightieth annual commencement of the Louisiana State University and Agricultural and Mechanical College, that E. Alan Swallow, as his name appeared on the program, was awarded the degree of Doctor of Philosophy. In August he was certified as a member of Phi Kappa Phi honor society by the LSU chapter. In the meantime, he had accepted an offer to join the faculty of the University of New Mexico. It was back to the West for Alan Swallow, and he would remain there for the rest of his career.[31]

4

Stern Critic

The Swallows drove to Powell for the summer of 1940, taking with them in the car the printing equipment, the new type, and Alan's plans for the Fitzell book. Arriving in Albuquerque in the fall, he discovered Hazel Dreis, who was enjoying a growing reputation as a bookbinder from her studio in Santa Fe. She prepared a case binding "at as low a cost as she could," which was $202, and the book came out in the fall.[1]

He always thought the Fitzell book, in blue ink on grey paper, was one of the best printing jobs he ever did, but his effort to market it taught him an interesting lesson in publishing. Entering a bookstore and showing the book to the proprietor, he was asked, "My God, why do you waste your time publishing this sort of thing?" The bookseller then offered to show him some publications he could "make some money with." The books turned out to be pornography, which the entrepreneur thought would sell particularly well "with the boys going into the army so fast." It was, said Swallow, "a good object lesson to have right at the start of my publishing work."[2]

With the move to Albuquerque, Alan Swallow's professional career took other steps forward. Although still an LSU graduate student working with Warren on his dissertation, he was a faculty member at New Mexico, teaching freshman English. There he met Horace Critchlow, a graduate student who was both older and wealthier than he and who shared his interest in printing. Critchlow bought a Chandler 10x25 press as well as type and other equipment that an Albuquerque resident had used as a do-it-yourself printing plant in the basement of his home. He and Swallow rented a garage near the campus, pooled their printing equipment in it, and went into business as Swallow and Critchlow. During their six months under this imprint, they formed Big Mountain Press, which did such printing jobs as a letterhead for a church, a leaflet for a plowboys' ranch, and invitations for sororities. They used a linotype they bought from a Baptist publication. Big Mountain, which would continue off and on throughout Swallow's career, later also produced "author's editions," charging a fee to the writer for publication and in some cases assistance in marketing.[3]

The aim of these commercial ventures was to enable them to publish serious literary works, which they began with a twenty-eight-page chapbook by Swallow called *The Practice of Poetry,* for which he received the same 10 percent royalty that he offered other authors. Under a new imprint, Sage Books, they published two regional works, translations of *Three Spanish American Poets* and an anthology of *Rocky Mountain Stories.* The anthology included a story by Vardis Fisher, whose work Swallow had read and admired as an undergraduate and would publish much of in the future.

Swallow took over the quarterly magazine *Modern Verse,* beginning with the issue of January 1941. In an editorial announcement he pledged "to keep his standard of selection catholic and broad, even though his journal's contemporaries seem largely to have become organs of groups or cliques of one sort or another, as much as anywhere in New York, the supposed literary capital of the nation." The issue contained poems by McGrath and Fitzell and three by the Stanford University poet and critic Yvor Winters that marked the beginning of a long and friendly professional relationship.[4] The third issue announced the inauguration of the Swallow Pamphlets, beginning with McGrath's *First Manifesto*.[5] The journal ceased publication after its fourth issue, which featured work by the rising American poet J. V. Cunningham as well as witty couplets by the editor's partner, Critchlow.[6]

Alan also became poetry editor of the *New Mexico Quarterly Review (NMQR),* which took over the subscription list of *Modern Poetry*.[7] Cunningham predicted the journal "could be made into a good thing if it can be kept going in these times."[8] Many little magazines were failing, and this became the fate of *Experiment,* a Salt Lake City publication formed by a cooperative group at Swallow's suggestion. He had been unable to find room for their work in *NMQR*. Alan Swallow would have much to do with a reincarnated *Experiment* some years later, and found room in *NMQR* for some of its work including "Car Hits Dog" by Carol Ely Harper, with whom he would have a curious epistolary relationship that would last the rest of his life. The first five lines of her poem give a fair sample of her literary style: "Here is the digging grace frozen clods up / O God great Universes Existences / Take care of him he is just like Mickey Poor

child Poor child Poor child / Screaming Bah cars splatter
blood points starred / Over pavement side to side arrow
red sawdust."[9] Ironically, in view of his apparent admiration for Harper's work, Alan would soon write that if
subjectivism as a literary method was followed to its ultimate conclusion it would leave the poet "the role only of
the recorder of the subconscious."[10]

The Swallow style was far different. One of the *New
Mexico Quarterly Review*'s first issues after Alan became
poetry editor included his poem "Journey," which begins
"Leaving the pines, the livid canyon," proceeds to "Coast-
ing the rolling Middle West," and ends "submarine, the
quiet air / Is ready to the tasteless tongue, / The beast
sits in it overhead, / And breath lies heavy in the lung."
There is also a story of his, "Man and Woman," in which
the woman, who is returning to an out-of-work husband
and is perhaps suicidal, has a brief encounter with a man
she notices from the sidewalk while he is working in his
garden. In the same issue, Swallow reviewed the *Poems*
of Yvor Winters and commented that "the fact that Mr.
Winters felt the need of printing the poems on his own
hand press is an unequivocal condemnation of the methods
of our publishers, who, pretending the 'literary,' refuse to
publish the best poetry written today unless baited in one
way or another, by fiction, by money, or, as Mr. Winters
says in the notes to the book, 'political maneuvering.'"[11]

In subsequent reviews Alan admitted that he could
not follow the poems of Dylan Thomas very well but
it appeared "that his complexity is a verbal one almost
entirely, masking a really uncomplex manner." He commented also on the "increased complexity and obscurity

of association" in the poetry of T. S. Eliot and called Robert Frost "a great minor poet." He noted that John Berryman, then beginning a distinguished career, was "worth careful reading" and would "profitably bear watching." Reviewing seven writers collected in a *New Poets* volume, he said John Ciardi, whom he later would disdain, stood out as "one of the most serious and competent."

Alan Swallow was already showing that he could be a stern and discerning critic. An anthology of war poetry was dismissed as a complex of "ineptitude, blarney and whipped-up patriotism" in which one poem by Wallace Stevens stood out "like fog lights in a winter night." A few years later he found "a terrible smugness and self-satisfaction" in Stevens's work. Swallow's mentor Robert Penn Warren was praised as "among the small group of truly distinguished poets of the United States," although one whose work had suffered by a loosening of structure. Richard Eberhart was "good, even provocative" but not top drawer; W. H. Auden had a voice of his own but had "written probably no more than half a dozen poems of really fine quality."

Alan wasn't sure where William Carlos Williams was going with the first volume of *Paterson* but there were "brief passages which are frequently fine and which may yet add up to an important major effort." Reviewing the second volume, he said it seemed "to embrace the wholeness of man's life," but regretted the loss of the "perfection of pattern" he admired in Williams's "shorter and slighter" poems. Similarly, he detected "a falling-off, both of irony and of memorable lines," in Ezra Pound's *Pisan Cantos*. Robert Lowell, he said, bowed too much to fashionable style but was "one of the significant talents among the younger poets."[12]

UNM faculty members knew their colleague as "a literate, even scholarly man" who seldom joked but would laugh uproariously and who "never outgrew the habit of solitude." At writers' conferences, he sometimes spoke so softly that he could not be heard in all parts of the auditorium. Often he would stand with his hands in his pockets. In one of only two published short stories that he ever wrote, the narrator speaks of his first love and says the experience left him "more alone, because more aware, than in any of his ignorant years."

As a critic, Swallow maintained that literature should be considered "as a proper study of its own" and not be approached from "some province outside literature proper" such as the history of ideas. To those like himself who were attracted by Marxist notions, he cautioned that important literature "should proceed from the material to the framework, emotional as well as conceptual, which explains it." Otherwise, he wrote, work that is "finely realized at the abstract level" runs the risk of failing "to give body to the abstract conception, to give thought bones, flesh, and blood."

As a publisher, he was an idealist whose books "would be tested by his own standards, not by sales, reviewers or the opinion of the New York publishers." Except for the Big Mountain Press works, he always paid a royalty to his writers, although he was not above asking them to chip in to pay for advertising, as long as the payments were directly to the printer and not to him. He was dedicated to the publishing of quality writing, especially poetry, at prices that he could keep low by doing much of the work himself.[13] He disdained "the modern manner of 'fine editions,'" saying that he published books "as a step in another process."[14]

Of work, he had plenty. Persisting in his leftist politics despite the warning of a University of Wyoming friend that he risked "a doctrinaire freezing of the mind,"[15] he sent an article about Marxist literature to his former LSU teacher Robert B. Heilman for criticism. He wrote an appreciative article in the *Rocky Mountain Review* about Winters, who thanked him for demonstrating "one virtue very extraordinary in contemporary criticism; that is, you appeared to have read the work you were talking about." The critic could not forbear, however, "talking as an English teacher" and cautioning Swallow to stop splitting prepositional phrases. Winters also warned Swallow that his publishing plans were too ambitious for his own good and would leave "too little time for your profession, let alone anything else." "Don't get involved in too professional a publishing venture, especially at your stage, or you will get nowhere," he wrote. He enclosed several poems for Swallow's consideration.[16]

A little over a month into his teaching stint at UNM, Swallow wrote to Winters, who had sent him a hand printed collection of poems "as one amateur printer to another." He could not think of a new volume, he said, until the Fitzell book made some sales, but he was sure Fitzell would sell well enough to cover the minimal costs. He had printed 200 copies, of which 150 were for sale at twenty-five cents a copy, with a royalty rate of 10 percent of gross sales. Presuming all 150 books sold at his price and not at a discount, the author would make $3.75 per book, or \$56.25. Winters had proposed some poetry collections, and Swallow said he should be ready to start a new project in the spring. He then went on to make it even more clear that he had no intention of heeding Winters's advice to steer clear of professional publishing:

> My publishing terms, so long as I can publish books at all, are as follows: a commercial edition of sufficient quantity to meet the demand, priced low enough that price will not constitute a great hinderance [*sic*] to sales (I am publishing Fitzell's collection, a large one, bound in half-cloth, at one dollar per copy), a royalty of 10 to 15 percent, a dozen or so author's presentation copies at no cost, and no financial responsibility upon the part of the author. Advertising will be such as I can afford, mainly in the form of notices and circulars to a considerable mailing list I have accumulated.[17]

The publishing partnership ended when Critchlow was drafted into the army in 1942. The departing partner took his printing equipment, leaving Alan with the handpress and type cases he had brought from LSU. Cunningham told him, "if you can keep going with the hand press, you can pick and choose more, and keep a thin trickle of interesting work flowing."[18]

By May 1941 Swallow was looking into an opening to teach American literature at Southwestern University in Memphis. In 1942, however, he accepted an offer to be an associate professor teaching English, journalism, and debate at Western State College in Gunnison, Colorado.

In his one year at Gunnison, Swallow did indeed keep the handpress at work publishing poetry, with occasional aid from hired printing. He also continued as poetry editor of the *New Mexico Quarterly Review,* winning praise from Fitzell for "turning it into a really good literary review, in fact one of the best in America."[19]

Gunnison was a bituminous coal town, and the Swallows got used to the glare of coke ovens and the snorting of locomotives hauling coal cars on the Denver and Rio Grande narrow gauge railroad. In addition to this nuisance, the school had restrictions that they may have found onerous. Its president didn't approve of smoking, particularly by women. The men got around the rule by lighting up in the faculty restroom, and Mae said that "if you'd stand outside the window you'd think it was on fire." When she smoked in their apartment, they pulled the shades.[20]

On January 4, 1943, the Swallows' only child, Ida Karen, was born. Like her father, she would be known by her middle name rather than the first name she had been given in honor of her grandmother. Ida Kate Swallow, who had brought the family to the Powell Flats, had died in September 1941, after a heart attack at the house in Powell where she lived alone. The day of Karen's birth was sunny and bitterly cold. Two weeks later, the temperature would drop to thirty-four degrees below zero, the coldest of the year. Four feet four-and-four-tenths inches of snow would fall during the winter months of 1942–43.[21]

The country was at war, and Swallow would soon be in uniform. He had passed his army physical in December and expected to be classified A-1, or subject to immediate call, in the draft. The college was seeking a deferment for him for the rest of the school year, but he thought

17. The Swallows' only child, Ida Karen, was born on the sunny but bitterly cold day of January 4, 1943, in Gunnison, Colorado, where Alan had accepted a teaching post after a stint at the University of New Mexico. Photo courtesy of Karen Swallow.

it would be "difficult to make out a case for an English teacher being in a critical occupation." A friend, responding to a letter from Swallow, wrote, "I have tried to think of some angle to work on for you, but . . . in your present occupation you are expendable." In a poem, "For My Infant Daughter," he wrote, "Dear child, I grieve for your birthright / Beneath these heavens: see, this year, / how

18. This picture of Karen was taken on her second birthday, after Mae and their daughter had joined Alan at Camp Grant, Illinois, where he was in training for army medical service. Photo courtesy of Karen Swallow.

blind, how deep the wound and scar" and concluded with the hope that peace and justice "yet may fall / On you, dear woman worthy grown, / On me, grown worth your backward look."[22]

As a member of a college faculty that varied from twenty-one to thirty-four during the Depression and war years, Swallow would have had a salary somewhere between $2,300 and $2,700 a year. The college, founded in 1911, had about four hundred students but the military draft was beginning to cut into enrollment. A history of the college described Swallow as a popular English professor who did considerable writing. A college official speculated that his female students might be the more likely to remember him "since he was (1) a writing teacher and (2) not a bad looking young teacher" although on the stocky side.[23]

In his journalism capacity, he was an advisor to the student Press Club. Continuing his literary career, he edited *American Writing: 1942,* published by the Press of James A. Decker in Decker's grandfather's drugstore in Prairie City, Illinois. The magazine published stories by Walter Van Tilburg Clark, Robert Penn Warren, and Eudora Welty, and poems by John Berryman, John Ciardi, J. V. Cunningham, Randall Jarrell, Robinson Jeffers, Stanley Kunitz, Theodore Roethke, Muriel Rukeyser, Yvor Winters, and many others. One reader said, "It's too bad the printing job couldn't have come up to the quality of the material, but I suppose Mr. Decker's merit as a publisher may be allowed to offset his weakness (here) as a craftsman."

In May 1942 Swallow signed a contract for his first book of poetry, *The Remembered Land,* but publication was delayed when Decker's grandfather died and the publisher took over the drugstore. Decker had twenty manuscripts on hand, and Swallow's was placed fourteenth. Decker then went into the army. *The Remembered Land* appeared in 1946. In the meantime, a pamphlet called *XI Poems* was published by the Prairie Press of Muscatine, Iowa. Alan paid $15 and received forty copies of the pamphlet. Publisher Carroll Coleman said he didn't like the idea of a writer's having to subsidize publication, but "if I am to continue to publish poetry there seems to be no alternative."

As a poet, Swallow was traveling in good company. In April 1943 his poem "A Day in 1942" appeared in an international literary issue of *The Old Line* at the University of Maryland along with work by Chile's Pablo Neruda, Welsh poet Vernon Watkins's distinguished poem "The Collier," Scotland's Hugh MacDiarmid, Spain's Federico Garcia Lorca, and American William Carlos Williams.[24]

Swallow was not a stranger to Gunnison's mountain campus, having first visited it in 1936 as a member of the University of Wyoming debate team. Before taking up his regular teaching duties, he served as a poetry critic and lecturer at the school's summer writers' workshop, as he would again the next year. He had told Mae that he wanted to teach in a small college where students would have small-town and farming backgrounds. "Being a Westerner at heart, I'm glad to be teaching in a school that has the true spirit of the West," he told the student newspaper, the *Top o' the World,* named for Gunnison's altitude of 7,681 feet. His publishing was "practically a hobby," he admitted.[25]

Swallow edited a *Top o' the World* poetry column called "Skyline" that reprinted a wide range of poetry. In one issue might be the first-prize poem in the Fine Arts department of the Colorado Federation of Women's Clubs. It could be followed in the next issue by John Crowe Ransom's classic "Dells for John Whiteside's Daughter." Swallow's own career as a poet reached a milestone in November when his "Ode to Russia" appeared in the prestigious *Poetry* magazine of Chicago. The poem contrasted "the field / Where daisies stood, where sheep moved low in clover" on his father's farm to a landscape where "The Soviet airman eyes the fields of dead." In his role of publisher, he brought out a small first book of poems by Ruth G. Van Horn of the English faculty at Western Michigan College and a collection of war poems, *Lament and Prophecy,* by Californian Ruth Forbes Sherry.[26]

As director of debate, Swallow supervised intramural competition in which teams representing fraternities and sororities met in the college's Little Theatre. They debated whether "the United Nations should establish a permanent federal union with the power to tax and regulate international commerce, to maintain a police force, to settle international disputes, and to enforce such settlements, and to provide for the admission of other nations which accept the principles of the union." Some readers must have been confused when one issue of the student newspaper described the question as whether "the United States should establish" such a union.

As the likelihood of being drafted with a wife and small daughter at home approached, Swallow explored the possibility of deferments. In March a friend who was already in the army wrote him that it was a "choice between this and the farm," agriculture being an essential occupation eligible for deferment. In August Alan was offered a position teaching Army Air Corps trainees at Montana State University, but no deferment was offered with it.

He was inducted in the October 1943 Selective Service draft call. Mae took ten-month-old Karen to Powell and moved into the home of Alan's parents.[27]

A skin condition, apparently an aftereffect of childhood acne, disqualified Alan for overseas duty. He reported to the Fort Logan, Colorado, reception center and worked as a substitute interviewer there for three weeks. In November he was reassigned to the Medical Department for basic training at Camp Grant, Illinois. The following

April he was named clerk of Company D, 26th battalion. Lt. William F. Black, commander of his platoon, said reports from noncommissioned officers indicated Swallow "has been trying hard to be a good soldier" and that his "pleasing personality has made most everyone he meets a friend." Shortly afterward, he was honored as "Soldier of the Week." During his stay at Camp Grant he was sent to a school held at Washington and Lee University in Lexington, Virginia, on educational reconditioning, or helping soldiers who had returned from the war to adjust to civilian life. Meanwhile he continued his editorial work with the *New Mexico Quarterly Review.* He found himself hampered in his literary pursuits because, of necessity, he had stored his books in Gunnison.[28]

Mae came to Illinois with him, bringing Karen, then just over a year old. The Swallows lived in housing off the base. When Alan was assigned to Madigan Army Hospital at Fort Lewis, Washington, as a technical sergeant in the Army Medical Corps, Mae returned to Powell but visited her husband. After Karen was two years old, Alan was transferred to Letterman Hospital in San Francisco to work at educational reconditioning. The assignment involved broadcasting over speakers to the soldiers and taking them to various churches and to see the sights of the city. "He knew San Francisco better than the natives," Mae said.

There was also occasional duty at Hoff General Hospital in Santa Barbara, where the Swallows bought a trailer house that they moved to what Mae called "a little cove in a trailer court" between Brisbane and South San Francisco. Alan hitchhiked daily to Letterman. A visitor to the trailer recalled lively discussions of shared political opinions. As often as they could, Alan and Mae went on weekends to San Jose, where they could show their daughter off to Alan's great aunt Charlotte. Alan wrote to an acquaintance that Mae was "a splendid and capable wife." A part of the proof, he said, was that she had stuck with him for nine years. "Although she has no particular interest in literature, she helped me with the publishing work, and she has suffered by being left to her own devices while I worked night after night at the press or the typewriter."[29]

In February the Swallows attended a family reunion in Powell. His father, recently discharged from the Seabees, arrived a day before him. Edgar Swallow had not served in World War I when he was a young man. He had had children and, like many others, had been needed on the farm. After the attack on Pearl Harbor, he decided, "I'm in the bank now and I'm not needed anywhere, I'm going to the war." He was assigned to Hawaii, where he found his duties mostly "cleaning the beaches, tin cans and stuff." He obtained an honorable discharge because the dampness of the island aggravated his rheumatism. His heart problems also were considered.[30]

When the atomic bombing of Nagasaki and Hiroshima brought the war to an end, Alan Swallow was hopeful he would stay out of the army of occupation in Japan and that demobilization of the men with families would be speeded. "I feel I have too much to do outside to fritter my time away, now, in the army," he said.[31]

In October 1945 he received a telegram that his sister Virginia, Mae's redheaded high school friend, was very ill in a Billings, Montana, hospital. He was given an

19. Edgar Swallow, who missed military service in World War I, enlisted for World War II after the Pearl Harbor attack and was assigned to Hawaii with the Seabees. He donned his navy uniform for this photograph with his son during a family reunion in Powell. Photo courtesy of Karen Swallow.

emergency furlough, but she died, at the age of twenty-seven, before he arrived. Hers had been a hard life. Words like "aggressive," "rambunctious," "fiery" were used to describe her. At eighteen she had married a farmer who turned out to be a heavy drinker and was not well liked by her family. She became ill with gall bladder trouble in 1941 and was treated at the Mayo Clinic. According to the family, the Mayo doctors delayed surgery because of her weakened condition and urged her not to get pregnant for a year. After the year, she did, and had twin girls who died shortly after birth. When he put together a collection of unpublished poems in 1942, Swallow dedicated it to Vera and to the memory of Virginia.[32]

During his army service in California, Alan Swallow continued his correspondence with Carol Ely Harper. Their first letters had been about the poems she submitted to him as an editor from her home in Walla Walla, Washington. In one of his first letters, on November 1, 1944, he said he found them "somewhat bawdy," but was considering some as a small collection. Harper was older than he, old enough to have a draft-age son. After his duties took him to Fort Lewis in December, Alan wrote that he wished they could have met while he was in the Pacific Northwest. The following month, headed toward Fort Lewis again by rail on the Portland Rose, he said that he "for one compulsive moment, had a notion to telegraph you to see if you could get off to come down to Pendleton and I'd stop off for a day." She wrote that his letter made her happy, and he said he was sorry he did not act on his impulse. From Fort Lewis, he wrote that, though it would be a long trip from Walla Walla, he would "like it indeed" if she came to visit. After reporting for duty at Hoff, he wrote, "I had come to look forward to our meeting. We would have liked and have enjoyed each other. I know that now! Well, so pass in the day and the night those things which gradually emerge into the often stupid consciousness as thoughts and desires. Perhaps another time it may be possible." The letter ended, "I feel I left something unaccomplished during my stay in Washington." He had told Carol he would like to meet her husband. He also said, "I hope you will show *this* letter to no one."

By 1946 Carol Harper was sounding Alan Swallow out on publishing a book of poems by her son, but he was cool to the idea. He was also unenthusiastic when she proposed an autobiographical novel or two about life in Walla Walla, although he conceded they might be publishable.

With the end of the war approaching, Alan turned down a chance to go to officers' training school. He was looking to the future, hoping to arrange a "hook-up" with an established publisher rather than continuing on his own. One publisher showed some interest. He also thought of a possible cooperative publishing house to be run in conjunction with *Experiment,* of which Carol Harper had just been elected assistant chairman.

Carol wrote asking Alan to describe himself, and he answered, "Usually quiet and self-effacive [*sic*] because of some adolescent experiences." In an earlier letter, he had said he liked "bawdiness in literature" as "an ape and a mock, a relief from some tensions." Then, asked what he liked to do, he answered, "Make love, work with mechanics, sometimes write," but "do none of these as well, I suppose, as I might; I am both lonely and gregarious." He found himself "getting a little fat" and "far from handsome" with his blond hair getting a little darker each year. He did not mention his calm blue eyes. He would like to get similar information from her, he said.

The letter was signed "cordially." At some later point, difficult to determine from their often scrawled exchanges, she metamorphosed from "Dear Carol" to "Carol, Dear" and eventually to "Darling."

In October 1945 an attack of kidney stones put Swallow in the hospital and he saw "some chance I may get a medical discharge." By mid-November, he was still in the hospital but getting daily passes that allowed him to leave. His kidney was functioning, but the stones were still there, and a doctor advised against removing them. On November 28 he was discharged from the army at Letterman. He saw "some chance of a job in California somewhere." Carol wrote a letter of recommendation to the chairman of the English Department at Berkeley,[33] and New Mexico had shown some interest in having him back. He and Mae stayed for a while with friends in Santa Fe, who had a typewriter he could use to start making more contacts. Then the Swallows headed for Powell.[34]

Their stay in the old hometown was short. When Swallow received an offer to fill in teaching English at the University of Denver in the final months of the 1945–46 academic year and for part of the summer, his plans to take the trailer to Arizona and write a novel were laid aside. "I've always thought I would do it some day, but so far that day has seemed a long way off," he said. The book was never written. By early 1946, Swallow was on the job in Denver and said his work there had started so well that he might not wish to leave. "Denver has some advantages, some disadvantages," he told Carol, "and I've made all my arrangements so far so that I'll be free this spring and summer to accept what seems to be the best spot I'm offered for a more or less permanent job." He thought of establishing a writers' colony in the Rockies, but wrote that it would take capital that he didn't have.

At this point, the idea of a newspaper career again entered Swallow's life, only to be quickly dismissed. Carol wrote him of plans for a new daily in Pasco, Washington, near the then-secret atomic bomb project at Hanford. Her husband, Maurice, was involved in plans for the paper. Her letter revived, Alan said, "my old feelings of wanting to do some good in the world through journalism" and the appeal of small towns such as the one he grew up in. However, he felt that "my profession is that of editing and publishing books" and that writing and publishing while running a small newspaper would be "very nearly impossible . . . so you see that I must still feel that I should not change horses now." Carol was disappointed, writing that she would like "to have persuaded you into Hanford after the war so you'd be within speaking distance."

The Harpers later moved to Pasco, at the confluence of the Columbia and Snake Rivers. The town was then gorged with sailors because of a wartime navy base. Carol wrote an unflattering poem about the town that was published in *Commonweal* magazine and said she was pleased to "have accomplished something for humanity at last! (Something besides writing of love!) Do you have to have reached maturity and been astonished often by love to be amused by love?" In the margin, Alan wrote, "Yes, I think so—and poems about it, too."[35]

5

The Biggest City Around

D espite Alan's hesitations, his sister Vera believed he had always wanted to make his life and career in Denver. It was a reasonable assumption. An ambitious boy from the Flat would very likely aim at the big city, and Denver, although still called by one writer "a good cow town," was the biggest city around, whose population of 287,861 in the 1930 census would grow to more than 300,000 by 1940.[1]

After his discharge from the army, Alan joined Mae in Powell, but not for long. Their Buick coupe had three jump seats on which they piled baggage to make a bed for Karen. The Denver offer was no longer temporary. Alan Swallow had received an appointment as assistant professor in English.

They had so much trouble finding a place to live that Alan was on the verge of leaving. Finally they found a dark basement apartment, the only sunlight coming from window wells. It was partly furnished and did not have enough room for all their things and no place to store them. Some had to be left in Gunnison.

There was difficulty with the landlady, a widow who would give treats to Karen after the four-year-old had been told by her mother, "You cannot have anything to eat before dinner." The landlady's youngest child was stealing, and Karen learned to steal too. When they tried to discipline her, she would throw a tantrum and beat her head on the floor. Mae said they would just "walk out on her, and she quit it." Finally Alan's parents came from Powell and said, "You've got to get out of there."

After more than a year in the apartment, they found the house they wanted. On York Street in University Park, a quiet neighborhood within walking distance of the campus, a developer was building eight houses, and they picked out a small two-story brick. "We came to visit weekly and sometimes all they had done was swept the floor," Mae recalled. "Oh, it was agony, waiting to get in." The house would be their home for the rest of their lives.[2]

Alan taught creative writing and contemporary literature, and started a summer writing workshop that grew into one of the first degree-granting writing programs in the country. There was correspondence with Iowa State Teachers College about a possible teaching job and with LSU about returning there to teach. "I could always have moved at a good increase in salary when I taught, as I am a good teacher and was in demand," Alan said, but he wanted to remain in the West. Besides, from his arrival on the Denver campus, he had been intrigued by talk that the university might establish a press. Because of his publishing background, he was urged by the graduate dean and the head of the English Department to come up with a plan.

After consulting with others on the faculty, he joined Professor Lawrence Senesh, who was mainly interested in the press as a medium for graphic art, in writing a detailed proposal and winning the approval of the administration.

20. Alan accepted a temporary teaching position at Denver University for parts of 1945 and 1946. After he received a permanent position as assistant professor in English, the Swallows bought this two-story brick house on York Street. Mae Swallow stands in front of what would be their home for the rest of their lives. Photo courtesy of Karen Swallow.

Alan became part-time editorial director of the University of Denver Press in 1947, while continuing to teach. The new sideline was at that time one of the few university presses west of the Mississippi River. The others were at Southern Methodist University in Texas and the universities of Oklahoma, California, Minnesota, New Mexico, and Nebraska.[3]

The East dominated the publishing scene and tended to look down on western writers. One dismissive review of a book by Idaho novelist Vardis Fisher was headed "Strictly from Idaho." The New Mexico writer Frank

Waters believed that the East "still regards the West as a backward province, suitable enough for a summer vacation, but far from the current of contemporary thought." The Easterners may have had a point. Given the West's celebrated wide open spaces, the market for books was bound to be skimpy. Consequently, publishers were few. One of the few was established by Caxton Printers of Caldwell, Idaho, a town that even a decade later had only about six thousand people in a state with fewer than half a million. Caxton, founded in 1927, was strictly a job printing company until it opened its publishing division in 1929. "We were one of the first publishers west of the Missouri River," Caxton editor Wayne Cornell recalled years later after the division's name had been changed to Caxton Press. The idea was that western writers were getting short shrift and Caxton wanted to give them an outlet.[4] Novelist Wallace Stegner wrote that "no press such as the Caxton Printers has a sales organization equipped to sell enough books to make publishing commercially profitable."[5]

Nevertheless Caxton persisted, and Alan continued to publish poetry and occasional fiction. His former partner Critchlow was in Denver, and they joined forces again, finding what had been Critchlow's press in the basement of a Unitarian minister, Rudolph Gilbert, who printed church bulletins and programs with it. Alan arranged to use it, along with his small handpress at home. He had help on printing, folding, and shipping from students. Marketing was tough, and Alan was soon convinced that "poetry does not sell to any considerable audience in our culture." His experience with "advance guard" booksellers added to the problem. One well-known one owed him for sixteen months, "enough to buy composition for a new book of poems." In 1948 he and Carol Harper formed the Experiment Group, a cooperative that published *Experiment* magazine.

The Swallows held occasional open-house gatherings at which students met such visiting luminaries as the poet J. V. Cunningham and Chicago's James T. Farrell, author of the then-popular Studs Lonigan books, both in town for a writers' workshop Alan was moderating. From the meetings at the Swallow home, ostensibly autograph parties for the authors, the students gained what one of them called "a sense of connection with the world of achievement."

Karen Swallow, not yet ten at the time, would later remember the York Street gatherings, remember sitting at the top of the stairs and attending, no doubt puzzled, to the adult conversation, with her mother most likely wearing one of her favored black dresses and people "coming up the stairs to read to me." Karen took a particular shine to novelist Janet Lewis, and enjoyed a ride into the mountains with her parents and their visitor.

Among the students was John Williams, a janitor's son from Wichita Falls, Texas, who went on to teach at the University of Denver for thirty-one years and win the National Book Award with his novel of the glory days of Rome, *Augustus.* At the Swallows' house, Williams learned to print and often operated Alan's press for him. His first novel, *Nothing but the Night,* was the first work of fiction Swallow published.

For bookkeeping, which Alan would never be very good at, and for proofreading, he had the assistance of Mae, who was also working at the university, as at LSU.

Even Karen, small as she was, pitched in, helping her parents carry books to the post office.[6]

With the partnership of Swallow and Critchlow resumed, they revived the Sage Books imprint they had started with three books in Albuquerque. The original idea had been to concentrate on regional works, but they had strayed as far as to publish a volume of translations of Latin American poetry. Now the two partners formed a small corporation called Sage Books, Inc., which published such titles as *Calamity Was the Name for Jane, Denver's Historic Mansions,* and *The Law Goes West.*[7]

These books were of uneven quality, often too long and marred by typographical errors. Alan acknowledged that in two years in the early 1950s he published only two that were good and sold well. But he felt the books filled a void, and once lectured an audience on the subject: "The History of the West: The Worst Scholarship in America." He felt strongly that "it is time we stopped apologizing for having an interest in the literature that comes from the West." Alan said later that the Sage books came to dominate his efforts "for the better, I believe." A bookseller said, "He knew western history was disappearing rapidly and he wanted to get as much in print as possible before it was forgotten."

To an unknown writer who asked if Alan would read his short novel, he obligingly agreed but asked for six weeks to get it done. He met the deadline, and told the aspiring novelist, "I'm sorry I can't get sold on this. There is much good in it . . . but I just can't agree that you have here selected the best technical methods of getting your story across."

The partnership with Critchlow ended in 1963, when the Californian moved back home.[8] In the winter of 1948–49, Raymond Johnson of Boulder, who had started his Johnson Publishing Company just two years before in his garage but had since moved downtown, approached Alan about joining forces. Working together, they expanded the firm's activities to include bookbinding and offset printing so that books could be produced under one roof. At the outset of the 1960s, the shop was turning out between thirty and forty books a year. Losses on the poetry books, however, were so great that Alan could undertake only those he could print with his own equipment, which meant four to six a year.[9]

Alan expanded the university's writing program to include a course limited to students working on book-length projects, resulting in the publication of at least three novels. His students frequently published poems and short stories in magazines and the once-tiny summer writers' workshop grew to attract as many as fifty-five participants. In September 1951 Alan announced establishment of a service to provide professional assistance to writers in the region. Novelist Frank Waters was among those helping neophytes with their manuscripts. Also established, after testing in Grand Junction, Durango, and La Junta, was a program of weekend writers' conferences at community colleges. On top of this, Alan was reviewing about sixty books a year until he gave it up almost entirely to concentrate on other work. *Denver Post* writer Alex Murphree said Swallow was "the busiest man we know and how he manages to do the work he does we'll never know."[10]

21. The Swallows added a basement study to their house and enlarged the living room. It was in this basement study that Alan's wife, Mae, found him slumped over his desk on Thanksgiving Day, 1966, dead of a heart attack at the age of fifty-one. Photo courtesy of Karen Swallow.

Alan received no increase in pay for taking on his duties at the university press. His teaching load was lightened to two-thirds, but not until after he had continued teaching full time for a year. Professor Senesh's interest in graphic art dominated at the beginning. The first works published by the press, from its office on the seventh floor of the library building, were not books, but posters designed to be displayed on school walls: "Help Yourself to a Good Research Paper" and "Where to Find

Facts on Federal Bills and Laws." These were followed by five UNESCO posters that were sold to the State Department for $10,000 and displayed in the department's centers abroad. All operating costs for the press were reluctantly paid by the university's bookstores for the first two years, after which it had its own budget but was still not showing a profit. University presses had not yet ventured into the more popular works that were the province of trade book publishers, so the Denver offerings mostly had such titles as *1947 Labor Relations in Denver Manufacturing, Foundation for World Order,* and *Exterior Ballistics.*[11]

In May 1946 the Rockefeller Foundation awarded Alan a twelve-month, $2,500 Post-War Fellowship in the Humanities to complete collections of his poetry and criticism and write a short critical and biographical book on Daniel Defoe for a series on English novelists. The situation became complicated. Alan wanted to interrupt work on the fellowship to teach during the spring semester. The foundation said this interruption was not allowed. Alan said he could not devote twelve continuous months full time to the fellowship and keep up his obligations to the university, to say nothing of the salary.[12]

After some negotiations, the foundation agreed. Then Alan accepted an offer to teach "The Theory and Practice of Contemporary Poetry" during a summer session at the University of California, which would net him more than his Denver salary. Again there were questions about whether he would be able to devote full time to the fellowship, particularly in view of his publishing work. Alan said he could keep up the publishing because it was spare time or hobby work and he lost money at it. In a report to the foundation, Alan said he had made progress on the Defoe book and the collection of criticism, but little on the poetry.[13]

Early in April 1948, at his home in Powell, Edgar Swallow Jr. had a heart attack so severe that his doctors sent him to the hospital. Alan was summoned home, as was Vera, then living in Billings. Edgar rallied, and the physicians told Alan it would be safe for him to return to his teaching duties in Denver. Later that month, the man Alan had long ago saluted as the "Precursor of poets you should have been" died of coronary thrombosis at age 52.

In addition to the grief it caused him, Edgar Swallow's death complicated Alan's professional life. His mother was named executrix of the estate and, although he said he would assist her when he could, he assured the Rockefeller Foundation that this would involve very little responsibility and would not interfere with his fellowship work. However, he said, it would require him to be in the Rocky Mountain region in the fall to deal with the estate. Teaching in Berkeley the second half of the summer instead of in Denver in the first, he argued, would enable him to devote himself to fellowship work in the fall. This reasoning was greeted with understandable skepticism at the foundation's West 49th Street headquarters in New York. "I am not clear about your situation in the autumn," John Marshall, associate director of the foundation, wrote. "Will your time then be completely free for work under the terms of the fellowship?" In the end, they agreed to split the remainder of his stipend into four equal payments to be made from September through December.[14]

Her father's death came at a troubled time in Vera's life. Her marriage to Ansel Walters, a restless man who was unhappy as a farmer, had been an off-and-on affair from the start. Twins, a boy named Ansel Edgar and a girl named Ann Evonne, were born to them in September 1941. They divorced shortly afterward, but soon remarried and moved to a farm near Laurel, Montana. A son, Bill Lester, was born in July 1945. Shortly before Edgar's death, Vera had started proceedings that led to her second divorce. At Alan's suggestion, she moved to Fort Collins to continue her education, taking her mother and the three children with her. Alta, forty-eight at the time, lived in the northern Colorado city for the rest of her life, enjoying bridge and other card games with new friends.[15]

There had been no Phi Beta Kappa chapter at the University of Wyoming when Alan attended, but one was formed after his graduation, and he was inducted into it. In May 1948 he had the honor of being invited to the chapter's annual honors banquet, but his name was misspelled as "Allen" on the program.

His health, never sturdy, was becoming more worrisome. The kidney stone was troubling him again, and he had it removed in February 1948. While recuperating, he had "a set-back [sic] to my heart" and was hospitalized for four weeks and given sick leave for the winter quarter.

In that year he launched a magazine, *The Advance Guard,* a guide to serious creative and critical writing in books and pamphlets. At first he intended to limit the publication to the so-called "little" literary magazines. By the time of its first issue, he had pragmatically concluded that promotion of serious literature required going beyond the noncommercial publications. His announced aim was to list and describe "all new publications . . . which, by as good a judgment as possible, may be classified as serious creative and critical work." In 1948 this effort was expanded to include an annual index of contributions to the leading little magazines. Its second issue inaugurated a column of editorial comment by the editor or others.[16]

In 1949 Critchlow and two partners purchased *Author and Journalist* magazine after the previous owner died. Alan agreed to edit the magazine in return for a share in the Author and Journalist Company formed by Critchlow and his two partners, Raymond Johnson and David Raffelock of the National Writers Club. As part of the deal, Alan had the use of a rented building, into which he moved the press that had been in Gilbert's basement. With handier access to the press, he produced two books of advice on writing. Two years later the magazine was sold to Topeka publisher Nelson A. Crawford and Alan found other storage space in a student's basement and a rented garage.

A contract with the Library of Congress in 1949 to publish its *United States Quarterly Book Review* enabled him to build a three-car garage-like structure in his backyard, with a long work table along the left wall and his handpress to the right of it, to serve as a press room. At one point he had books stored in this building and in two rented garages. With the radio playing on the windowsill, he would work there at distributing type, shipping, or printing. His automobiles were parked outside.

Alan was not long alone in his work. Gus Blaisdell, a former student of Yvor Winters at Stanford, was

22. Raymond Johnson of Johnson Publishing Company in Boulder, Colorado, and Alan Swallow formed a partnership in the winter of 1948–49 under which Johnson would use his equipment to produce books for Swallow. The partnership foundered in the early 1960s. Photo courtesy of Karen Swallow.

hitchhiking through Denver when Winters spotted him by chance and told him to look up Swallow. Blaisdell did, and stayed for three years, reading manuscripts and editing. The two of them might discuss favorite Swallow writers, experimental work Alan had seen in magazines, the latest sports car or motorcycle news, and, in the spring and summer, how the horses were running at Denver's Centennial track. The *Quarterly*'s editor, Joseph P. Blickensderfer, sought "lively but cool" unsigned reviews of about 250 words, and enlisted more than 400 experts to review 510 books in the publication's first year. Alan served on the quarterly's twenty-member advisory committee. In June 1956 the financially pinched library discontinued the publication. Alan offered prepaid subscribers a subscription to the Swallow Press quarterly *Twentieth Century Literature* in its stead.[17]

Alan also established an imprint entitled The American Fiction Library, to reprint such works as *The Invasion,* a 1932 novel by Janet Lewis, dealing with American Indian life. The idea was a series on "aspects of the culture or cultural development of America." During a stopover in Santa Fe, Alan had learned that *The Man Who Killed the Deer,* a 1942 novel by Frank Waters about an Indian community, was out of print. He checked it out of the library, read it "with admiration and respect," and wrote Waters asking him if it was available.

It was, but there was a hitch. In the time of Pearl Harbor, few readers had been interested in American Indians. The metal plates for the book had been contributed to the war effort so were not available. By the war's end, the book "had become a collectors' item, but only Alan Swallow had enough faith in it to reissue it," said Waters. The reprint sold no better when Alan took over publication through Swallow Press. Although the book was later available in paperback and in illustrated limited editions in Germany, France, and Britain, its sale was disappointing in the United States. It was not until the 1960s, when the cause of Native Americans became fashionable, that the book really caught on.[18]

It was Alan's declared policy to pay his writers a royalty, however small, without any financial contribution
from them. In a rare departure from this standard, he and
Critchlow agreed to accept money from Carol Harper to
guarantee actual costs of *Big Bend,* her book-length poetry
manuscript about the Columbia Basin region of Eastern
Washington. A selection of the work had been rejected by
another publisher as "unfinished, the material for poems
rather than poems." Alan had reservations about the book
himself, thinking it would not sell, and he did not "have
the money to sacrifice" on it. He would rather have kept
the financial arrangement secret, but in the end said, "Let
them think as they wish . . . anyone who knows anything
about my work knows I am not a vanity publisher."

To combat "the vicious practice of vanity publishers,"
Swallow and Critchlow set up a printing-for-hire facil-
ity, under the Big Mountain Press imprint, with authors
retaining all rights for the books they paid to have printed.
"He was wise enough to keep those areas separate which
a lot of small press people aren't," a fellow publisher said.
A typical arrangement was an offer to publish a history
of the Episcopal Church in Colorado for Allen D. Breck,
chairman of the History Department at the University of
Denver, at a price of $1,975 for five hundred copies.[19]

Later, when Vardis Fisher proposed to assure publication of his *Testament of Man* series by buying copies of the
books, Alan at first "was tempted . . . to tell you to go to
hell with the plan," but finally accepted it as an invest-
ment in a joint venture. In January 1961 correspondence
between Fisher and Swallow showed the author paying
$4,000 for the printing of his *Orphans in Gethsemane.*[20]

In tandem with his work at the university press, Alan pressed on with his idea that some of the Swallow volumes "might well make a go of it on the commercial market through a joint arrangement with a New York publisher." In May 1946 an arrangement was made for joint publication under the imprint The Swallow Press and William Morrow & Company. Morrow provided the New York outlet, with Swallow in editorial charge. Among the first titles to appear under the new imprint were critical works by Yvor Winters and Allen Tate.

Unfortunately, the writers with whom Alan Swallow worked were not found commercially feasible in the New York publishing scene; they did not sell enough to justify the expense. By the outset of 1947, Alan said he "would now bet 50–50" whether the arrangement would last. An October 1948 financial statement from Morrow bowled him over. The books weren't selling, and his capital was exhausted. He had gone back to printing his own books, but that wouldn't pay off for another year. In 1951 the agreement was dissolved.

The experience had a significant effect on the course of Alan's life. When the deal was made, he abandoned previous thoughts of moving to a new job and determined that he would remain in Denver. He tried at least to make another change. As he did with his students, he tended to befriend his authors and advise them on their problems. "Now that my responsibilities are greater, with a larger publishing program, I must be more and more wary of it," he told Carol Harper. "I've learned, even from your case, that I can't do it, Carol."[21]

The Morrow venture also led Alan to briefly expand his publishing enterprise to the Philippine Islands. Morrow had a representative for Asia and the Philippines, and through that contact Alan became interested in a manuscript by N. V. M. Gonzales, editor of the *Evening News Magazine* in Manila and a novelist whose *The Winds of April* had won the Commonwealth Literary Contest in 1940. *Seven Hills Away,* twelve mystical stories of the Philippines by Gonzalez, was printed in Denver and published simultaneously in Manila by Halcon (cq) House, coedited by Swallow and Gonzalez.[22]

For any publisher, the years after the war were not good ones. Fiction sales plummeted through 1947, and publishers responded by trimming their fiction lists by 288 titles, or 15 percent, in 1948. To Swallow, this cutback spelled difficulty for the serious beginning novelist. At a conference at Idaho State College, he said, "I question very seriously whether the first novels of some our present successes—Hemingway and others—would have been accepted" in the climate of the early 1950s. His plan, he said, had been that by relying on his own labor, he could make sales cover other expenses, and it had worked, but only "approximately." As a press grows, he said, "one must still use all devices possible to substitute work for money" and find other people willing to contribute their labor.

As for poetry, he found his experience with publishing it so discouraging that he thought, "Perhaps poetry does not offer a mode of communication, in this and future cultures, which can survive." Nevertheless, he said, "Next to survival of mankind, survival of poetry and art seems to me most important; indeed, survival of mankind without poetry is the survival of a humanity of which I would not wish to be a part." In a newspaper interview, he found Denver "a quickly growing literary center" although "still producing too much third-rate stuff." He urged young Rocky Mountain poets to "stay here," saying too many became discouraged and left. Faced with such a situation, he "tried to make an integrated work out of teaching, out of editing and publishing, and, with what energy might be salvaged, out of writing." But in five years, he wrote only criticism and one story, and was anxious to get back to poetry. The writer Mark Harris, a student at Denver while Alan taught there, said, "His publishing struck me as crazy. He published poetry and criticism by people I had never heard of, assumed financial losses, and was constantly in search of warehouse space for thousands of books he never sold."[23] As a teacher, Alan was "on the verge between assistant and associate professorship" midway in his first year as a full-time faculty member. And besides, he said, "with my fairly quick tongue and fairly ready head, it provides more extra-curricular time than any other profession I know"—certainly more, he thought, than journalism. Certainly his mind was ready for what came, but some would disagree about the "quick tongue." "Among fellow professors and talkative students," Mark Harris said, "he was slow at repartee and banter, giving the impression of a man either humorless or a little deaf."[24]

He was candid in criticism. A friend recalled seeing a student approach him with a manuscript and ask what he thought of it. After looking it over, Alan said, "This is very bad, son." "Should I keep at it, sir?" the student asked. "Not unless you want to give your life to it," Alan replied. In his writing classes, he would read a student's work aloud "in a detached voice, without emphasis" and without identifying the writer, and then ask fellow students to criticize it. When he asked one of his better students why he broke the lines in a free verse poem where he did, the student answered, "I say the words over and when I think they feel right, I have the line." Alan commented that "it was clear that he had no real principle for making his choices."

Whether teaching contemporary literature, Shakespeare, or the English romantic poets, "his eye was for the page, and his ear was inner," and he demanded that the student "read not the person but the text." Many of his bright young students rebelled against the method, arguing that the writer should show his devotion to social change. But, said Harris, "I began at last, in the classroom of Alan Swallow, to learn to hear and read." Although Mae later said that she always wanted to sit in on one of his classes, she never did.[25]

Outside the classroom, Alan had not abandoned the political activism of his college days. For a publisher who had begun his career by publishing the always leftist Thomas McGrath, the Red-baiting crusade of Senator Joseph R. McCarthy and his supporters brought new strains. Alan found time to be active in the American Civil Liberties Union, of which he would become Colorado state chairman. In three years as his student, Mark Harris found him "a political radical . . . when such radicalism took much courage." He supported Henry A. Wallace's Progressive Party campaign for the presidency in 1948 and

was one of the few professors at the university who spoke
out for the right of students to campaign for Wallace.[26]

As a poet, Alan Swallow was encountering disappointments. In 1942, just after entering the army, he had assem-
bled a collection, *The Remembered Land,* with a moving
poem "For Mae" ending,

> It will not matter that the earth, or sky,
> Or any sea are never ours alone.
> It is enough that we can turn an eye
> Upon the world and see the sun on stone.
> It is enough that we can see the night
> Come down, and will not feel the need of light.

The book waited four years for publication by the Press
of James A. Decker and was little noticed. For the later
War Poems of Alan Swallow, reviews were for the most part
disappointing. An anonymous hometown reviewer in the
Denver Post saluted the "integrity and simplicity—without
posturing" of such quatrains as "What shall we say for
those who lost / In many lands many a brother? / They
settle meekly under frost, / And like dead leaves cover
each other." The classical scholar, translator, and poet
Dudley Fitts, however, writing in the *Saturday Review of
Literature,* said the writings in the book "deal with the
war, it is true, but they are not poems" and "only occasionally rise to the level of competent verse . . . Mr. Swallow's Pegasus is strictly horse." The reviewer in *Poetry,*
Sherman Conrad, found much of the work "run-of-the-
mill," yet said it offered "an experience of a very certain
magnitude, or quality quite un-ordinary in recent war
poetry." Conrad said the poems, which included "For My

Infant Daughter," "find their way through many denials of extravagance into one's esteem. Their prospects grow."[27]

The University of Denver Press, meanwhile, was encountering hard times. When it remained in the black, this was owing to support from the university. As director, Alan constantly battled to make the press a going concern, but in April 1952 he asked to be relieved of the responsibility and returned to full-time teaching. In September, the administration decided to close the press, a decision described by one local journalist as a "lamentable execution." When the actual shutdown occurred on August 31, 1953, the balance sheet showed $48,000 in income and about $55,000 in outlay. Indiana University Press took over the two best selling of the press's twenty-one titles, a pair of drama anthologies edited by Eric Bentley. A few others were taken over by authors or small publishing firms. By borrowing money and making "some long-term arrangements with the university," Alan secured some of them for his Alan Swallow and Sage Books imprints.

On February 25, 1954, Chancellor Chester M. Alter announced the resignation of Dr. Alan Swallow as associate professor of English at the University of Denver. For the first time in fourteen years of publishing, he had found himself making a little money from it and concluded he "couldn't keep up both teaching and publishing and do either well." From now on, as he had envisioned as a teenager in a Montana service station, he was to make it on his own as a publisher.[28]

6

Alan Swallow, Publisher

Alan Swallow's venture into full-time publishing was a gamble. After thirteen years of combining publishing with either teaching or army service, his press was earning a little money that he could draw on, and he decided to "let it have a full chance for a time, to see what would happen."[1] Gross income for 1960 was about $100,000 and payments to authors were close to $20,000. Swallow was by no means sure what the outcome would be. "I've always felt that I cannot publish the things I want to publish and make a living, however poor a one, considering family obligations," he said.[2] At first he talked of giving it two years, concentrating chiefly on regional titles, and then "quit it, pull it down arbitrarily to a few things, or hire some labor to help carry it on" and return to teaching somewhere. Seven months into the project, he was "really knuckled down, living almost in a world of my own,"[3] a description his family would find increasingly apt.

After nearly two years, Alan told an acquaintance in 1956, the case was "very much up in the air." He could always go back to teaching, "but when and if I do, I'll have to cut the publishing back to a smaller thing that I can possibly manage part-time; now I can't manage it full-time!" "Relative 'success' is harder to bear sometimes—well, all times, than when I was doing fewer, selling less," he complained.[4]

Mae switched from part-time to full-time work at the university, mostly so that they could provide a college education for Karen, and she and Alan hired an African American maid to look after the home. Sometimes the maid would bring her grandchildren over and they had what Karen recalled as a social life together. The maid did all the housework, but Alan often cooked lunches and dinners. The meals were repetitions of the same three or four because "the focus was on the work so cooking had to be practical and fit in."

Shortly after Alan embarked as a full-time publisher, the man in charge of trade publishing for a Madison Avenue text and technical publishing firm asked him to scout manuscripts for him. The man had been trained in advertising, and so had most of his staff. "So . . . he had to come up with books into which these high-powered men could sink their teeth" and produce "enough income to pay their high-powered salaries." The man told Alan he would like the books to be good, but "goodness or badness was not an important criterion in his judgments." Alan, as always concerned with getting and keeping quality work in print, was "personally pleased that this firm never made as much in trade publishing as they apparently thought they would." Too many people in publishing, he concluded, "do not really like books and know nothing about them in a quality sense."[5]

Swallow's small press had entered the field at a time when the giants were experimenting with paperback publication. The cheap paperbacks, Alan felt, were "brilliant and useful" at offering literary classics at low prices but had "not demonstrated the equally important ability to put us in touch with the best developing work of our own contemporaries." After initial reluctance, he entered the higher priced paperback field in the late 1950s because "with a backlist of some very fine work, I felt an obligation to the work and to the authors to try this newly developing market for them . . . Perhaps we need to coin a new term and speak of 'little publishing.'"

In an article in the early 1950s, Alan wrote,

> Both the short-range and the long-range conditions for publishing are deeply, deeply disturbing. It is hardly possible to think that our literature will be defeated by complete commercialization into the cheap and shoddy, or that, in another long-range development, "serious" books would need to be charitably "sponsored" and the commercial publisher deteriorate to the level of the commercial magazines; yet, like atomic warfare, conditions for this grisly prospect confront us each day as we go to our literary labors.[6]

Tending to his literary labors, Alan intended at first to concentrate on poetry, except for the regional titles, believing that a small press would be unable to market fiction adequately. His New Poetry Series offered royalty publication, through a contest, to poets who had not previously produced a book. The series brought out first books by Vi Gale of Portland in 1959, and Joan Swift and Nelson Bentley, both of the Seattle area, in the mid-1960s. His Swallow Paperbooks in Poetry published Edith Shiffert's *In Open Woods*.

From 1953 to 1959, he published six issues of an occasional periodical, *PS,* the title standing for poems and stories. It was frankly "a personal magazine for the editor and his friends, and the work they feel ought to be given a hearing."[7] In fiction, he found himself more and more taking on "extremely fine work which was not being done by the large houses"—books by Janet Lewis, Vardis Fisher, Allen Tate, and others.[8]

"The last months of 1956 were nearly too much for me; I really got in deep, and I'm not through with the mopping up work even yet . . . I'm so damned far behind financially . . . and I had to borrow rather heavily to get

23. Poet and critic Yvor Winters and his wife, the novelist Janet Lewis, were both Swallow authors. Winters and Lewis were occasional visitors to the Swallow home, where Lewis was a particular favorite of young Karen. Jose Mercado/Stanford News Service.

by the last two or three months," Alan said.[9] In April 1957, trying to recoup, he toured Texas in the Jaguar XI20 convertible he had bought secondhand, complete with two crumpled fenders, and restored. His weeklong series of lectures netted him $400.[10] He also inquired about getting an income tax deduction by donating some of his correspondence to a library.[11] When word circulated that the Swallow press was being sold to New York publisher Roger Strauss, he feared the false rumors would damage him with booksellers and reviewers.[12]

There were, of course, intervals of relaxation at the horse and car races that he loved. He would come back from the horse track and tell the family about his day. He

24. A lifelong automobile enthusiast, Alan bought this 1957 Jaguar XC120 convertible and made a lecture tour of Texas in it. The Jaguar, he said, was "pretty much a man's car." *Denver Post* photo.

was doing well enough financially that he could afford to lose $300 at a crack, provided he made it up on other days. Naturally he liked the stock car races, noise and all. Karen thought he would have tried to be a driver if it had not been for his doctor's advice and Mae's reluctance.

Other evenings, they would go to amateur baseball games at Observatory Park in their 1932 Chrysler. The former taxicab had a window between the front and back, and Karen and her girlfriends would sit in the rear seats while her father was in the park umpiring a game. He wanted to restore the Chrysler to the glory of its taxi days, but gave it up as too expensive.

At basketball games he would rush to shake hands with the players, his midsize frame dwarfed by their towering

25. Despite his busy publishing and writing duties, Alan Swallow found time for occasional family picnics. Alan and Mae share the right bench, while Karen stands in front of an unidentified guest. Photo courtesy of Karen Swallow.

height. His daughter remembered his buying English cars, including a Raleigh for her mother. Later there was an Austin. They always had three or four cars at a time, but never a Cadillac. Swallow detested Cadillacs, saying they were designed by groups of people and not by individuals—perhaps an echo of the contrast between the New York publishing houses and his own.[13]

He would race around Denver in a convertible sports car delivering the books he had published.[14] His teenage passion for motorcycles also revived, to delight and plague him. He bought a powerful bike that his daughter thought "almost too heavy for him to manage" and later turned it in for a smaller one that was easier to start. In November 1957, driving the vehicle in Denver traffic, he turned to change lanes just as an automobile driver was doing the same. He came alongside the car, and it caught and twisted his leg, requiring splinting, a pin, and repeated operations. "Nip-and-tuck about loss of my leg from the calf down, for a time," he said. To make matters worse, he developed eye trouble and diabetes, which Karen thought he would have avoided without the stress of the injury.[15] The accident nearly caused serious injury to his knee.[16]

By January, still in a cast and on crutches, he resumed printing in the garage by standing on one leg. A second cast, "as big as the first one," was put on early in February.[17] "Still crutches for some months, apparently."[18] He was back in the hospital for Memorial Day. Doctors took three chips from his hip and grafted them onto the break in his lower leg.[19] A month later, he said the leg had "not been comfortable at all since the surgery."[20] By August his doctor was allowing him to do limited driving with the cast on.[21] In October he was back in the hospital. Only two of the three bone chips grafted on to his leg had lived, and a low-grade infection had developed. Doctors removed the pin and a section of skin and flesh, and at last allowed their patient to substitute crutches and a brace for the cast.[22] By January, in the midst of Denver's most severe winter in years, Alan defied his doctor's warnings of a possible damaging fall and tried walking about the house with only the brace.[23] To make matters worse, Mae wrenched her back in June and was still in "much misery" on the Fourth of July.[24]

At home, Alan liked to eat standing up and to drink inexpensive whiskey.[25] The family traveled frequently to New Mexico, a state Alan was fond of from his days in Albuquerque.[26] Often they would visit with Lorraine and Harry Pearson, who were Karen's godparents.[27] Years later, Karen found this incongruous, as her father "was really an atheist or had come to the point where religion and reading of religious materials was a waste of time." Alan was careful, however, not to offend others with religious beliefs. When an editor handling a manuscript for him suggested cutting prayers and other religious passages, he told the editor to eliminate "only that which offends readers and duplicates." Nevertheless his attitude, Karen said, "just gave starvation for me." She joined the Episcopal Church and her father embarrassed her by going to sleep when she took him to Christmas Eve service. In her life and career, she would study philosophy and religion intensively.[28]

Karen, like her mother, seldom wrote letters, but spent part of each summer with her maternal grandmother in Powell. For the girl, the visits were a time of "being in the country, and going to the fair and just playing." She remembered flying up from Denver and then her parents picking her up for the trip back in the Jaguar. Alan's mother had fallen into a deep depression after the death of her husband, and Karen avoided her company. The treatment for depression at the time was electric shock, which was briefly considered but vetoed by Karen.[29]

Karen recalled Alan as "kind of a devoted Daddy" who "liked babies as much or more than lots of men."[30] On her graduation from junior high school, her father said fondly that she was "a pretty good kid in most ways."[31] However, she said, "I know really that he wanted a boy because a boy would have been more likely to have taken over the business. I'm sure it was in his mind from the very beginning."[32] Vardis Fisher had the same idea, but Alan denied it, saying, "I don't feel any need that my particular work, in itself, go on."[33] Karen, feeling that her talents were not literary, took a class or two in art and would always remember how much she loved them. Alan let her illustrate one book, *The Charcoal Horse* by Edward Loomis, when she was not yet in high school. "He was trying, I think, to work with one of my talents," she said, but "it became hard" and nothing came of it. As her father's health deteriorated, she thought this situation became more difficult for both him and her.[34]

By himself, Alan kept doggedly at work in the hardest times. On crutches after surgery on his leg in the summer of 1958, he would dash out to the shop to stand working at packaging, but have to give it up after twenty minutes to go back in the house and elevate his leg. Karen was home for the summer and was, he said, very attentive and helpful. "The whole house was structured around his work, really," she said.[35]

Swallow's collection of his own poems, *The Nameless Sight,* which he had originally planned to call *The Inward Sight,* was published in 1956 by The Prairie Press, then in Iowa City, Iowa, to reviews much better than those that had greeted his first work. The New England poet John Holmes detected a sensibility "with pity and hope for the nameless and the named, in the war, and the campaigns of time." Swallow's poetry, Holmes said, was "not easy to touch . . . because he is preoccupied with man's stern endless struggle." Holmes's assessment in the *New York Times Book Review* ended, "Like a Saxon warrior he stands, as it happens in Colorado, doing what he must do while he can, stand up."[36] In Denver, poet and journalist Thomas Hornsby Ferril said Swallow's poetry was "characterized by formal precision, fluid compactness, with no ambling imagery."[37] Swallow met with some raised eyebrows, including perhaps his own, when he reissued *Nameless Sight* as a Swallow Paperbook in 1963. "I have had a policy not to publish my own things" and "that is why I hesitated," he said. "The general principle . . . is still as sound as ever, and is the one to be obeyed."[38]

Continuing his political activism, Alan was a member of the Colorado branch of the American Civil Liberties Union in the early 1950s, at the height of the anti-Communist furor that came to be known as McCarthyism. Shortly after resigning from the University of Denver, he looked back on his years as a liberal in academia and mused that a battle was being waged between the traditional view that a student should achieve "some result already

known, already premised for him" and the idea of allowing the student "to arrive at conclusions, attitudes, and
ideas according to the nature of pertinent evidence." A
decade later, as chapter chairman, he led the group in taking a strong stand for abolition of the House UnAmerican
Activities Committee and personally favored abolishing
the Central Intelligence Agency as well.[39] Swallow always
argued that the chapter should concentrate on being an
action group, and felt that about 80 percent of the time
spent on membership and educational activities was wast-
ed.[40] In municipal politics, he joined a citizens' committee
supporting George A. Cavender, Democratic president of
the Denver City Council, in his unsuccessful campaign
for mayor in 1959. About the same time, he became president of the Colorado Authors League.[41]

In 1957, in collaboration with some former students,
Alan started a magazine, *Twentieth Century Literature,* "to
have something which would return to the basic things
about discussing the literature, rather than the pattern
established by the literary quarterlies." The quarterlies, he
said, were espousing the kind of reasoning and "taste" that
he had been taught in graduate school and now rejected.
He hardly ever read them.[42]

He hired no salesmen, arguing that they would raise
the break-even point on a book by at least a thousand
copies. He paid $150 for an ad in the *New York Times Book
Review* and was unable to trace a single sale to it.

On at least one occasion, he considered acting as a
literary agent, telling Vardis Fisher that he would like to
represent him in that capacity on a proposed book Fisher
had outlined during a visit to York Street.[43]

In a self-assessment about this time, Alan said he was not "an old, world-weary, fed-up guy" but "quite energetic and most of the time optimistic—if not philosophically so, that is, convinced of a benign universe, practically so."[44]

7

Alan Swallow and His Authors

As an editor, Alan Swallow worked slowly and carefully, spoke briefly and bluntly, and was, in words of poet Vi Gale, "very adamant about what he would tolerate and what he wouldn't." He edited word by word, comma by comma, scribbling marginal notes that were so hard to read that Gale thought he must have hurt his hand in his motorcycle accident.[1] Reading one prose manuscript, he found that he was managing only thirty pages per hour. One writer noticed that as he discussed a manuscript with him he seldom made "any gestures of those strong, almost stubby hands."

Some of Swallow's writers did not appreciate the close scrutiny. The poet and critic Yvor Winters complained to him about "green ink on the galley sheets" for a collection of his poetry. "You took it upon yourself to revise three of my poems with disastrous results," he wrote. "Please return these passages to their original lineation; it was correct in the galley proofs and was correct in the copy I sent you. These are my poems."[2]

Gale, too, did not always agree with Swallow's editing. "He tended to push me into a kind of formality that I was trying to break out of," the Portland poet said. "And he thought that stuff ought to be rhymed, and I had tried to break away from that."[3]

When a manuscript entitled *Displaced Persons* was submitted to him one summer day in 1956, Swallow wrote the young poet Don Gordon that he liked the work, but publication would not be until several weeks into 1957. He also said that after a careful reading he felt that "the collection needs some selection." When the time came for specific cuts, he proposed eliminating nine poems altogether and editing out the second pages of two others. This amounted to about one-fourth of the original manuscript. "I realize I have been pretty severe," he told Gordon. "Think over the suggestions. I shan't kick too hard at the admission of a few—a very few."[4]

Swallow could also be severe with authors of prose. The New Mexico novelist Frank Waters was a fluent writer who found that "the words flowed easily from my old Parker pen."[5] Alan considered him sometimes "bull-headed" and thought his work could stand condensation. He persuaded Waters to condense an early trilogy about western gold mining—*Below Grass Roots, The Dust Within the Rocks,* and *The Wild Earth's Nobility*—into one novel, later published by Ohio University with the author's changes. Oddly, Waters, much unlike Winters and others, thought Swallow did not edit his books at all.[6]

The politically leftist Swallow called Thomas McGrath, whose poetry he had first published while still at LSU, "possibly the only poet of the Left in America worthy of serious consideration alongside the distinguished Left poets of Europe." This opinion did not stop him from wielding his editorial pencil.[7] He continued to publish his old friend's work, but with reservations. Working with McGrath on a collection in 1964, he told him that

26. Alan Swallow considered Frank Waters's classic novel *The Man Who Killed the Deer* "darned near as much my book as Frank's." In his old age, Waters believed he owed his career to Swallow. Photo copyright Cynthia Farah Haines.

some of his recent poems were repetitive, "pretty cruel caricatures of your style" and, in short, that the volume would require deep cuts because his current output was so disappointing.[8]

With writers he found just plain inept, Swallow could be truly harsh. He told one woman who had submitted a historical work about Dodge City that "the writing is really quite poor" and "in some places you have been taking legend for history, or something near legend."[9]

Winters, despite his objections to some editing, said that while Swallow was not, in his opinion, a good poet and had "no gift for style in his work," he had "a remarkable sense for style in the work of others; he could read accurately and evaluate correctly."[10]

Like most editors and publishers, Alan Swallow was on the lookout for talent. Winters first met him when the future publisher, just discharged from the army, appeared at the Winters home in Palo Alto "wearing a uniform which looked as though it had been through the entire war." The Stanford professor said Swallow "had a way of telephoning without warning, appearing for an hour or two and then disappearing into the night." Such meetings led to publication of many Winters works, both poetry and prose. The poet had turned from experiments in free verse to a formalism that was increasingly unpopular among critics but admired by Alan Swallow. Despite, or perhaps because of, his virtues, Winters was, as Swallow once observed, "disliked in many poetry camps" for such unorthodoxy as saying that the little-known Elizabeth Daryush was America's foremost living poet or that Edith Wharton a better novelist than Henry James.

Swallow's judgments, too, sometimes went against the grain of literary fashion. He turned down a collection by Josephine Miles, a California poet who later won coveted awards with poetry influenced by Beat movement poets such as Alan Ginsburg. Also rejected was a book-length narrative poem by the more conservative Winfield Townley Scott that was snapped up by New York University Press.[11]

Swallow first spotted Vi Gale's work in the *New Orleans Poetry Review* and encountered its author at a University of Colorado writers' conference in Boulder. As he was walking into a campus theater with a lecturer who was to speak, his companion pointed out Gale, who was earning an academic reputation for her work in fiction as well as poetry. Both waved to her, but Gale thought the "stocky gentleman" accompanying the lecturer intended only a friendly gesture. When she got back to her dormitory, she found a note from the lecturer saying his companion was Alan Swallow, who wanted to talk to her.

Too shy to call Swallow on her way home through Denver, she went back to work on a poetry collection. By 1957 she thought it was finished, so she sent it to him with a note saying they had "met on one occasion, almost." Swallow wrote back saying the collection was not ready for publication, but it would be. After working with her until he was satisfied, he published it as *Several Houses.* The book received good reviews and sold well. When Swallow published her second book, *Love Always,* it contained several of the poems she had agreed to take out of *Several Houses.* "Either he was changing or I was changing or he was tired or we were both tired," she said.[12]

At first Swallow concentrated on poetry, arguing that a small publisher should not do fiction. Later he declared the fiction business "most interesting" and told Allen Tate, "I kept doing some as I found extremely fine work which was not being done by the large houses."

Among the works he cited were Tate's Civil War novel *The Fathers* as well as work by Janet Lewis, Vardis Fisher, and Frederick Manfred. "I don't think that considering the time interval (seven years in business at that time) and the quality and the fact of not just reprinting chestnuts of dead authors in new editions, any publisher could match that!"

While Swallow was at Louisiana State, Robert Penn Warren called his attention to a novel he admired, *The Invasion* by Janet Lewis. Alan shared, and continued to share,

Warren's enthusiasm. Lewis based her novel very largely on documents of a mixed white and Indian family in upper Michigan. It was a method she used again in court-case novels such as *The Wife of Martin Guerre.* Swallow often handed this book to people, or recommended it, and said that he "never found one who did not admire the work, genuinely like it." Yet Lewis's books never became widely popular, nor won the critical praise he believed they deserved.[13]

After publishing Tate's novel, his book of critical essays written from 1928 to 1948, *On the Limits of Poetry,* and other works, Swallow felt sorry for its author. "The guy had genius," he wrote. "He struggled, rather badly and not independently enough, but without much comparative attention—not like his vast inferiors. The struggle destroyed him, and he went weeping. The work has some great value, but it is flawed; and meantime he is a mouse. He will not do another thing of any real value; indeed, he has not done any for more than a decade. He deserves pity."

Tate was a difficult personality whose closest friends often found him offensive. Nonetheless, Swallow was too harsh in his judgment. *The Fathers,* which had been quickly forgotten after it first appeared in 1939, deserved the recognition it received at Swallow's hand. Critic Arthur Mizener called it "the novel *Gone with the Wind* ought to have been." It tells a story of people who move back and forth over the Potomac River bridge linking northern Virginia to Washington and who find themselves enemies in the "foolish excitement of war . . . not knowing which beliefs were right and which were wrong."

Swallow first met the Parisian-born bohemian writer Anaïs Nin in 1947 when she and her new husband, Rupert

Pole, stopped in Denver on their way west to California.[14] She was to prove the biggest disappointment of Alan's publishing life. In 1961 he proudly announced Nin's addition to his list, describing her as "one of the world's most important writers." Nin had contacted Swallow because she saw that he was publishing Tate's novel *The Fathers.* Alan would bring out a new book of her novelettes, reprints of her stories, and the *House of Incest,* and take over from her one volume in print, *Cities of the Interior.*

Nin told him she would give him an option on her diaries. She qualified the option as "(for the future)," and later described it as "a gratuitous gift I made Mr. Swallow purely out of gratitude because he kept my books in print."[15] He had published her when other publishers would not, and she had been reduced to printing her own books and making meager sales because they did not get reviewed. She was soon complaining "that to be distributed by Alan Swallow was almost as frustrating as to be my own distributor. He could not get reviews except in college magazines." The only way she and he could get reviews was by making a friend of somebody on a newspaper, she said unfairly.[16]

Nin's royalties from Swallow for one year came to $270.[17] He, however, believed that her narrow readership would give way to a broader public, and he was right. *Time* put her *Collages* on its annual Christmas list of the best books of 1964, stimulating healthy sales during the holiday season. Then her agent was offering her work to New York publishers; possibly he knew that Swallow had been advised to curtail his publishing activities after his heart attack. At any rate it was a clear violation of Nin's agreement that

Swallow would at least copublish. Later he learned that the book that had been offered was Nin's lucrative correspondence with author Henry Miller, and that it was being published by Putnam. Alan told Nin that with deep regret he was withdrawing his agreement to publish her work. "I see no pride in publishing what I believe those books to be—trading upon Miller's name in one case, and emasculating (and it would be that, even if only 5% were cut out) the diary in the other case. I wouldn't want to publish such books." He said he would not accept the diary "if it is capitalizing on a version even slightly bastardized in order to get publication in a big time way right now."[18] "It probably would have been a big break," said Vi Gale.[19]

Of Frank Waters's novel *The Man Who Killed the Deer*, Alan Swallow once said, "Sometimes I feel this book is darned near as much my book as Frank's." He admired it as a "quietly assertive" study of a man caught between two cultures, an American Indian who had gone to a white-run school. Waters knew something about such conflicts. He had grown up in Colorado Springs as the son of a half-Cheyenne Indian whose Southern mother-in-law was "never quite reconciled to accepting him into the family."[20]

When Swallow republished the novel after it had been long out of print, Waters said that Alan's faith in the book gave it a new twenty-five-year lease on life, with editions not only in America but in Britain, France, and Germany. In his old age, Waters believed that he owed his career to Swallow. He found Alan a noncommittal man whose "placid manner never betrayed the nervous compulsion that made him drive his gray Jaguar at one hundred miles an hour"—speed at which Waters was "a little afraid to

ride with him." Swallow was, he said, a "rationally con-
scious man belonging to day" who "worked in the dark
unconscious realm of night." Waters tried in vain to get
him to modernize "the old-fashioned and dull-looking
catalogue upon which he relied to sell his stock."[21]

The first time Alan Swallow met Frederick Manfred was when "there appeared on my doorstep one day,
unannounced, this veritable giant." Manfred introduced
himself and said he wanted to talk about his publishing
problems. He had plenty. Manfred's early work, written
under the name Feike Feikema, was published by a small
Minnesota firm called Twin Cities, which had since gone
out of business. Under his own name, Manfred wrote an
autobiographical trilogy that invited, and received, com-
parison to Thomas Wolfe. Next came a historical novel,
Lord Grizzly, that would sell well enough to go into a
paperback edition.

His next effort foundered. *Morning Red* was a novel
about American Indians in the northern plains, and
Native Americans were still not a popular subject in the
literary marketplace. The book had been turned down
by McGraw-Hill, Knopf, and other eastern publishers.[22]
Although he had never met Manfred, Alan had read his
work. So, he asked, "When a man of genius stands before
you and says that his most ambitious, most important novel
to date won't be published by the New York houses, what
the deuce do you do? I did the only thing I knew to do,
and that was to publish it." The words encapsulated a publishing philosophy that won Alan Swallow much praise,
but eventually contributed to such heavy losses that he
concluded, "I just don't know how I can do more."[23]

8

Vardis

Alan Swallow rejected the first manuscript Vardis
Fisher offered him, without even seeing it. Meeting Fisher for the first time at a University of Denver
writers' conference, he told him he could accept no prose
books of any length as long as he was limited to doing his
own printing.[1]

Fisher was to become Alan's best friend among all
his authors. They disagreed over matters large and small,
but were bound together in part by childhoods spent in
barren patches of western land and by struggles to over-
come resulting shyness and perhaps well-concealed feelings of inferiority. "You have been a wonderful haven to
me, dear friend and brother," Vardis once told Alan.[2] "As
Fisher says, we are brothers," Swallow said.[3] According to
one account, vigorously disputed by Fisher's wife, Opal,
transactions between the two were often informal and not
put in writing.[4]

Vardis Fisher was a cantankerous, petulant, and preju-
diced individual who wrote off liquor as a business expense
and often talked of ending his life as a suicide bomber
who would kill only himself.[5] He was a heretical writer
who said that such Christian doctrines as original sin "are
a hospital, and the only people there are sick people who

27. Novelist Vardis Fisher was probably Alan Swallow's best friend among his writers. "We are brothers," he once told Fisher. In later years Fisher was a sharp critic of some aspects of Swallow's career. Grant Fisher and Special Collections Department, Boise State University Library.

don't want to get well."[6] A Northern Idaho librarian told him "that if she kept on reading my books she would go straight to hell." Another librarian publicly burned some of his volumes.[7]

During the Depression, Fisher battled bureaucracy and political censorship to produce almost single-handedly an *Idaho Guide* that was acclaimed as one of the outstanding accomplishments of the WPA Writers Project.[8] In personal appearance, he struck one young writer as "rather the romanticist's ideal of what a novelist should look like

and be: rugged appearance, long head, prominent fore-
head under thinning hair, alert brown eyes, and prominent nose and chin,—this above wrestler's shoulders and
arms, long tapering fingers and big feet."[9]

When Fisher's works made their first appearance, he
was compared with such literary lights as Thomas Hardy,
Theodore Dreiser, and Thomas Wolfe. In his depiction
of the Snake River country where he grew up, calling it
the Antelope Hills, he was said to have equaled Hardy's
Wessex or William Faulkner's Yoknapatawpha County.[10]
As time went on, his reputation so faded that he estimated
Swallow was selling forty or fewer copies of any of his
titles in a year and if he withdrew them, "I don't think any
publisher would want me."[11]

After the author's twelve-volume *Testament of Man*
series was completed, Swallow told him, "I think this
series must surely be counted one of the major literary
projects of our time, perhaps of all time." When the interview was reprinted seven years later, the hyperbolic statement was dropped.[12] Alan seems to have been alternately
enthusiastic and wary about the mammoth project.

He told Fisher that the reception of the series was
"going to get tough," particularly as it approached "the
precious Christian era." Nevertheless, he said, "perhaps
I ought to see what I could do about it."[13] Fisher's agent
thought Harcourt Brace would make an offer, and the
author was torn between the advantages of a big publisher
and his loyalty to Swallow. In the end, Harcourt said no,
and Alan told him, "We're in this together."

Swallow would be the publisher of the *Testament* series,
and Alan believed it would do well.[14] Like other eastern

publishers, Harcourt had balked at, among other things, the elaborate notes that Fisher appended. Alan agreed to them after Vardis argued that the notes were necessary to show that the works were based on scholarship.[15] Fisher and his wife, Opal, talked Swallow's offer over while getting "pleasantly stinking," and decided, "It will be a pleasure for you and for us. We like the idea."[16] When Swallow proposed to send out advertising under a special 1½-cent rate, Fisher replied that he got bales of such stuff every year and threw it away unopened. "I really think we should do our damnedest so that the envelopes will be opened, and once opened, the contents read," he said.[17]

As the books came off the press, there were disappointments. When Alan attempted to interest English teachers in the series, he found that "if they praise Vardis, it is carefully qualified with the qualification that, of course, it was former work, before he committed the big folly."[18]

Fisher's own agent, Elizabeth Nowell, told him that his *Goat for Azazel,* which followed *Jesus Came Again,* was "60% treatise and 40% novel." The book raised religious issues touchy enough that both author and publisher talked of sending separate advertising circulars to Jewish book dealers and Christian ones.[19] They settled on one for "religious" and one for "general" stores.[20] Alan said only one of the five hundred religious booksellers filled out the circular's order blank and returned it. When a Jewish reviewer gave *Goat* the cold shoulder, Alan told Fisher he was not surprised, because "you give the Jews hell in the book."[21] As the series neared its finish, the best the author and publisher were hoping for was to break even.[22] Three Jewish friends to whom Fisher proposed to dedicate *Goat for Azazel* "said no with thanks and in vigorous terms." "I guess I still don't understand how deep the hurt is in these people, for so many centuries of persecution," he said.

Although the books were fiction, they were indeed the fruit of substantial research. After the series was finished, Opal recalled how "supremely happy" he was when "wonderful books were sent to him by fine libraries all over the nation."[23]

Jesus Came Again drew disappointingly few reviews (Fisher said the only ones he spotted were in the *Chicago Tribune* and *Cleveland Press*), and sales were so poor that Alan figured he had lost $3,000 on it. When Fisher told Swallow that it had taken him a long time to realize how heretical the books were, Alan replied, "Yes, Vardis, they're heretical as hell." Heretical or not, he vowed to keep publishing them, even if he had to do the printing himself in the garage. They were monsters to print. Vardis Fisher was so wordy a writer that even he, appalled at the bulk of one of his manuscripts, photographed it.[24] When he got it to the post office he found it weighed fourteen pounds.[25] His *Orphans in Gethsemane* ran to more than nine hundred pages and half a million words. The manuscript weighed twelve pounds. *Children of God* was more than seven hundred pages long. Only two of his books, *April* and *Love and Death,* occupied fewer than three hundred pages.[26]

Things looked up with publication of Fisher's Lewis and Clark novel, *Tale of Valor,* in 1958. Dorothy Parker mentioned it favorably in *Esquire* and Idaho's Republican Senator Henry Dworshak agreed to take a copy to

President Eisenhower, who promised to read it. The record does not show whether he did.[27]

In 1960 Alan arranged with Terence Williams, a graduate student in library science at the University of Denver, to prepare a bibliography of Fisher's work. He said it was an important project and "should not hurt sales." The plan was complicated when he learned from Vardis that another man at the University of Idaho was already working on an exhaustive bibliography expected to take years.[28] (Alan at first thought he might publish both, but decided against it, and was annoyed that the Fishers had apparently given the Idaho scholar more cooperation than they gave him.)[29]

Orphans in Gethsemane was plagued by typographical errors. Even the name of the garden outside Jerusalem, where Jesus was arrested, was misspelled on the title page in the proofs. The error was caught and corrected, but many survived. Vardis was appalled, and Alan regretful. "I am going to have to get someone to read for me, I guess," he said.[30]

Looking back over his first thirty years of writing, Fisher said he averaged $750 per book.[31] When his novel of Mormon history, *Children of God,* won the Harper Prize, he used much of the $10,000 to buy property and build a house near Hagerman, Idaho, not far from the Eastern Idaho hamlet of Annis where he had been born. Life in Annis had been hard, his Mormon mother a "stern and unbending Puritan" and his father given to angry outbursts whenever crossed. In this dysfunctional family, to the accompaniment of beatings by a neighborhood bully, he grew to be known as "old irascibility" himself.[32]

Despite the coveted prize, New York publishers often refused Fisher's work and he fell back on Caxton Printers. When he agreed to sign copies of his latest novel at a Boise bookshop in 1956, only one person showed up, and that prospective customer did not buy.[33]

As a dedicated liberal, Alan found Fisher's deep-seated conservatism, displayed in his "Vardis Fisher Says" column in Idaho newspapers, "a source of serious amusement to me" and called him "the best political reactionary I know."[34] The two finally came together politically in opposition to the Vietnam War, which Fisher denounced as a "brutal slaughter of people" promoted by "damned ignorant war-mongers."[35] Alan thought of his friend Vardis as an intellectual novelist, unpopular in an age of "'guts' writing, like Faulkner and Hemingway."[36]

Ironically, Fisher had gained more literary recognition in the nation as a whole than in his home state. After his death in July 1968, the situation was reversed. His national reputation dwindled, despite paperback publication of the entire *Testament of Man* series by Pyramid Books, yet Idahoans began to pay attention to him. In June 1991, a monument to "Idaho's foremost native author" was dedicated at a rest area overlooking the Snake River Canyon near Fisher's boyhood home. *Idaho Daily Statesman* columnist Tim Woodward wrote a biography, *Tiger on the Road,* describing Fisher as "one of the most complex and unpredictable writers his region had produced." The movie *Jeremiah Johnson,* made from his novel *Mountain Man,* had its premiere in Boise in November 1972, with star Robert Redford in attendance. Governor Cecil Andrus marked the occasion by proclaiming Vardis Fisher week in Idaho.[37]

In 1995 a Vardis Fisher symposium was held at the College of Southern Idaho in Twin Falls, with folksinger Rosalie Sorrels singing and telling stories about "grumpy old Fisher."[38] In neighboring Utah, a quarterly magazine, *The Vardis Fisher Newsletter,* was inaugurated in 1990 in honor of Idaho's "unofficial state curmudgeon."[39]

9

Expansion and Collapse

When Alan Swallow's publishing enterprise reached its twenty-first anniversary in 1961, he was publishing about thirty volumes a year and one of them, the *Collected Poems* of Yvor Winters, had just won the $2,500 Bollingen Prize. The Denver Public Library marked the occasion with a display of several dozen of the more than 250 books Swallow had published.[1] He had become, in the words of Frank Waters, "a little one-horse publisher that was known all over the eastern seaboard."[2] He was acclaimed as "the only publisher west of the Mississippi to break the monopoly of the Eastern publishing establishment which looked down its nose at Western writers and books."[3]

Nevertheless, Alan still regarded himself as "a sort of teacher on sabbatical" in the uncertain world of small press publishing. "I certainly did not set out to make a living publishing serious poetry," he wrote. "I merely set out with determination to publish it honorably and to learn how I could do it without being stopped." As it turned out, he said, "the poetry over-all makes a few dollars" but his living came from the overall list.[4] He disdained the hat-in-hand appeals for money made by many little magazines as though "the world owes the little magazine publisher/editor a living." If an editor "can't make it on his own, he'd better shut up," he said.[5]

Alan printed some books on his handpress, and for the most part packaged, addressed, and mailed the volumes himself. He was known to go to work at 10 AM and sometimes work off and on until 4:30 the next morning, often smoking a pipe or cigar in a work space packed with books, correspondence, and manuscripts. The room had a big desk, a typing table, and a small cot.[6] The hours were chosen, Mae said, because Karen was asleep and the telephone was not ringing. Once Alan attended an evening Western Round Table meeting and then resumed his wrapping from 11 PM until 4 AM. In a typical year, there were about 70,000 copies to mail, about 5 percent of them to Europe. Alan usually reserved early afternoon hours for running errands.[7]

In spring 1960 the Swallows drove to Los Angeles, making side trips to San Diego and Santa Barbara. "Mae enjoyed it a lot, and deserved it a lot," Alan said. As for himself, he "even forgot about the publishing for a little bit." Back in Denver, he worked overtime at shipping and other chores for three weeks "to gain back the week lost."[8] He was, he said, "at the very edge of what I can do." Returning a manuscript, he told an author that "sometimes the old body just won't do what is wished."[9] The writer, Harry E. Chrisman, cautioned him that "you had better slow down since no book or books, mine included, are worth breaking your health or risking a nervous breakdown."[10] Alan himself said that what he did had "an almost suicidal drive to it, but I find that I can do the books I do, and since, for whatever reason this became the

Edgar
Alan
Swallow

1960

28. In 1960, when this picture was taken, Swallow returned a writer's manuscript with a letter telling him that "sometimes this old body will just not do what it wishes." Courtesy of Karen Swallow.

developed, self-appointed (if you will) role of my life, then I do them."[11]

On the last weekend in August, the Swallows visited Vardis and Opal Fisher at the log house Vardis had built outside Hagerman, Idaho, overlooking a lake he had also made, across a footbridge and up stone steps that he had laid.[12] Vardis's usual contrariness nettled Mae and bothered

Alan. "Vardis got pretty far off base at times in needling people," he wrote to the Fishers. "I can't quite figure out the purpose in it . . . If it is the novelist merely trying to get material for writing, it is understandable but not always excusable." Mae, he said, was "a solid person who ordinarily would have enjoyed the argument and discussion; but in that case there was hardly room for 'discussion' or 'argument' for your method did not permit it. I think that was her great frustration of the time and something new to her."

The argument may have concerned a statement Alan had made about female writers in a magazine article. He had written that "there are three women writers of fiction whom I admire greatly. By marking them off as women, I do not mean to suggest inferiority. Indeed, I do not believe I could name three living men writers of fiction who are their equals." Alan said this meant that he regarded the women as equal, but Vardis maintained he had said something "stronger" than that. He bet a good bottle of whiskey on it. Looking the magazine up after he reached home, Alan concluded that the article seemed to imply he could name only two living male writers as good as the women, so he owed Vardis the whiskey. Vardis asked him to send Frederick Manfred's *Lord Grizzly* instead. Alan said he and Mae "talked . . . a good bit" during their fourteen-hour trip about Vardis's cantankerous manner.

Alan showed his usual love for speed, revving the aging Jaguar X120 up to ninety-five on four-lane highways. He slowed to the sixty-five-mile speed limit only after spotting a highway patrolman as he approached Rawlins, Wyoming. Alan called the Jag "pretty much a man's car" and loved to drive it on highways, although he drove around town in his more sedate MG.[13] A few days after their return from Idaho, Mae received a letter, presumably some sort of apology, from Vardis. Alan said she "seemed to appreciate it" but probably would not reply, because she was not much of a hand at writing letters.[14]

Mae's assessment of Fisher and his work was different from her husband's. While Alan admired the ponderous *Testament of Man* series, his wife especially admired *April,* a short novel written mostly from the viewpoint of a lonely young woman on an Idaho farm dreaming of the "unpredictable mad designs" of the clouds and wind.[15] Her attitude toward Fisher was not unlike her view of many writers she met through her husband's work. "Mae is always pretty wary of authors," Alan said elsewhere. "She will generally start out with an opposed feeling, on seeing any new ones."[16]

Swallow's partnership with Johnson Publishing came to an end over differences with owner Raymond Johnson that cropped up early in the 1960s. Alan complained of delays in production of his books, saying at one point that Johnson had taken three weeks to do a three-day job. The trouble apparently arose because Johnson had outgrown Alan's small enterprise and taken on major projects that crowded Swallow books out.[17] A shortage of help may also have contributed to the delays.[18] At one point, Mae approached Johnson's daughter, Ada, about coming to work for Alan. Ada, in her mid twenties, turned the offer down. She had just gone through a divorce, had a baby to care for, and did not relish the idea of driving from her home in Boulder to Denver every day. Late in

1962, Swallow and Johnson agreed to end their association. Johnson's daughter said there was some kind of falling out, and she suspected it was because Alan had become
demanding.[19] Alan said things between them had been
on the point of breaking for some time.[20] The Canadian-
born poet Edith Shiffert, whom Swallow published, said,
"I don't think he angered easily, but stubbornly continued
at what he was doing."[21]

After the falling out, or whatever it was, Johnson
completed production only of the Swallow books that
were already in progress. This left Alan looking around
for other printers, some in the East and Midwest although
his aim was to keep the work concentrated in the West.
His Sage Books imprint was "growing like mad," generally outselling his literary titles, and "primarily, I suppose,
keeps me alive," Alan said. "The lit'ry game has its problems," he told Vardis, and he feared they would inten-
sify.[22] From some of his authors he withheld royalties,
writing on the statements, "PAYMENT TO BE MADE
ON DEMAND."[23] On the other hand, some high-priced
books in the nonfiction Sage line were selling well over
20,000 copies and he was taking on so many manuscripts
that he was always behind.[24]

Alan was thus forced to cut back the number of titles
he selected from the four hundred or so manuscripts he
was receiving in a year. Some were returned unread for
lack of time. The Sage imprint was doing so well that
Alan received an offer from a Los Angeles group to buy
it. The prospective buyers were "good enough guys in
their way," Alan thought, "but their whole background,
and approach, is publicity, public relations, etc."[25] From a

financial standpoint, the offer was attractive, and it would enable him to concentrate on the literary side of his publishing, "my first effort and first love."[26] Nevertheless, he decided against it, feeling "sure in my bones that inside a year they'd have run it into the ground."[27]

To writers whose work he wanted to publish but could not say when, he gave the option of either withdrawing their manuscripts or waiting an indefinite period.[28] Still, he was peeved when Vardis Fisher sent his manuscript of *Suicide or Murder: The Strange Death of Meriwether Lewis* to the University of Oklahoma Press instead of to Swallow.[29] After not hearing from Fisher for two months, he feared he might have offended him by complaining.[30] In the end, Vardis sent him the manuscript, and he published it.[31]

In the spring of 1962 the Swallow family's health problems intensified when Mae was hospitalized for a gallstone and gall bladder operation.[32] "Doing all right, but, lord, it does keep down the time so that even the routine has to fall behind a little bit," Alan noticed.[33] The summer was the worst he had ever had, and he found it unfortunate, in a way, that they had to make a trip to Wyoming over Labor Day. Karen would be home, so she could go with them. Although it was usually an annual pilgrimage, it would be the first time in two years that they had gone. Driving to northern Wyoming would take a lot of time, and in Powell there would be "a scurrying, etc. among relatives."[34] Mae's mother, on the other hand, thought Alan was "always so cheerful" and enjoyed everything on his visits.[35]

As the book business turned increasingly to paperback publishing, Alan predicted resistance from some of the specialist American dealers, but recognized the trend as a portent of things to come and declared that it "just has to be tried."[36] He arranged with Paper Editions Corp. to wholesale the books, but the arrangement turned sour. Their agreement was that invoices would be paid at a 50 percent discount within fifty days after a title was closed out. Alan found payment almost impossible to get, even under these conditions, and by October 2, 1962, "decided I had had enough" and withdrew from the agreement.[37] "The plight of the publisher in paperback is pitiful in many ways," he lamented.[38]

Alan's health was increasingly troublesome. On November 18, 1960, after an unusually busy session of packing books, he had undergone a hernia operation. On Christmas Day, while playing bridge during a family visit at the house of friends, he felt chest pains. His daughter recalled that he was reluctant to have a doctor called and "sort of sat on the stairs." When Mae got him home, she called the doctor. It was a heart attack.

While recuperating, Alan had to read manuscripts in bed and write letters to authors by hand. He also wrote a stiff letter to Paper Editions, which owed him $1,600, and received $500. Less than a month later, word came that the company was in bankruptcy. Alan expected payments to him would cover at most 17 percent of the retail price of the books. To James Schevill, one of his authors, he wrote, "I have had, of course, the normal concerns about the heart, and the additional problems that a three-handed guy feels when he has to work with two hands now."

When his health permitted, Alan Swallow was a popular speaker at Denver literary and historical functions. In

July 1960 he spoke on "The Influence of American Publishing on Creative Writing," which he did not think was
always good, at the twenty-seventh Writers' Conference
in the Rocky Mountains in Boulder. He gave a poetry
reading at the University of Denver in May 1961, and lectured on western Americana to the Colorado Historical
Society that same year.[39] He gave a Library Week speech.
He served as a Spur Award judge for Western Writers
of America.[40] He moderated a panel discussion on "The
Present Situation of the Poet."[41] He judged a Colorado
Day essay competition.[42]

Increasingly, such work was done to the accompaniment of pain. In mid–May 1964 he began to feel "muscle-
jumping and spasms and the like" in his leg "so that it can't
be ignored and puts me into the shakes." Soon he was
on three antibiotics plus painkillers. By July he was "just
mildly annoyed" by it and pretty much resigned to annual
recurrences.[43] By the end of the year, he was putting off
surgery "to a more convenient time."[44]

Understandably, he appears to have become more careless in business. When the publisher of poet James Hearst's
Limited View allowed him to use his composition work for
an offset reprint, the publisher stipulated that his name
not be used. When the book appeared with the publisher's
name on the back cover, he wrote a friend, "The company of honorable men, never large, daily diminishes, and
it saddens me. I did not think Alan would do that."[45]

In January 1963 Alan Swallow started bleeding and the
possibility of cancer was discussed. A doctor made tests
and was satisfied that nothing was seriously wrong. Mae,
apparently finding her husband a difficult patient, wrote

the Fishers, "He does seem to be improving. I don't know, of course, about the future. Maybe I'm not the one to help him with it. I wasn't successful in the past. I am trying to do my best, tho, so he will be less obstreperous."[46]

Within a week Alan was putting in a few minutes a day catching up with routine business at his typewriter. A printed postcard sent to authors and bookstores said, "Mr. Swallow has had a serious reversal in health. The office for both shipping and editing will be closed for a period of time." On a copy sent to Virginia McConnell in Colorado Springs, Alan said he was still reading manuscripts in bed.[47] However helpful Mae might or might not have been in dealing with his health problems, she obviously put her business school training to work on such matters as income tax. When the work became irksome, she observed that "in the next life she would become a lawyer to cope with that stuff."[48] In the meantime she also dropped her husband's letters into a mailbox on her way to work.[49]

In April the injured leg erupted into acute pain and required hospitalization. Nevertheless, to his wife's distress, Alan worked until four AM on mail, manuscripts, and proofs, and arose at ten-thirty or eleven to make phone calls and tend to a shipping boy "who needs a good deal of tending."[50]

He had been home from the hospital only two weeks when a young man from the Hearst Corporation flew to Denver and talked to him at his bedside about buying him out. The visitor proposed that Swallow run the Denver operation on a salaried basis while advising Hearst on its paperback lines. The reaction was ambivalent. On the one hand, Alan said, "I just don't visualize it. If I keep doing what I'm doing (and I wouldn't want it any other way) such as printing poetry myself, etc., I haven't time for advising them." On the other hand, "The only other problem is the health, how best to have things in case something does happen that puts us underground. In that sense, plus the wish once in a while just to relax from the drive to keep the thing working as it has, makes the sale an attractive idea, but only for a moment." There was no sale.[51]

"I still believe that the way of doing things is to have the conviction that one is doing good work, offer it as such without apologies, and fight for a market for it," Alan said.[52] The expense of changing printers, however, put him in a financial bind. When Vardis Fisher offered to help him by buying books, he was uncertain. "If you want to invest in copies, all right: that would be your decision; but you are not to do it out of pity for my situation; I am coming along all right on that, by dint of some pretty hard work."[53]

Alan had a severe attack of angina in September, but by January he was "breathing better and facing 1964 better."[54] He figured he had published "47 good titles" in 1963 but had such a pile of manuscripts on hand that he returned more than 250 of them in three weeks, "boiling and boiling down to the last ones for serious consideration."[55]

In the meantime, on a four-day New Year's trip to New Mexico, he and Mae joined Frank Waters at the Taos Inn for a few drinks and some paper hats and horn tooting. When they got back to their hotel, the leg was so bad that Alan paid a two AM visit to the hospital in Taos for a painkiller.

Alan doubted that he could "stall the doctors any more about surgery." He could not. By autumn 1964 the operation had been performed.[56] "The doctor whittled away quite a bit," he told Carol Harper. "I have about half the bone knitted. Still not enough to walk on and probably not enough for some time. The crutches still. But I am getting more and more mobile, and it will be better." His heart, meanwhile, had worsened. "Going to live a long time, I'm sure, but I do need to proceed with caution," he wrote. Arranging with Carol to print some Experiment Press books, he urged her to keep it simple because "if we can't . . . I don't want to do it; for it is extra work when I badly need to cut down."[57] By the fall of 1964, his leg forced him to cancel a planned trip to Oklahoma with Mae, and was "so damned bad, would sneak out" to the garage whenever he could stand it to fold pages.[58]

The long-distance personal relationship with Carol continued. He wrote her that he had been disappointed in *Experiment* magazine, which was being abandoned. She wrote back in distress, fearing the difference of opinion would carve out a chasm between them. Alan tried to soothe her feelings. He had been disappointed, he said, when a missed plane connection thwarted a possible get-together. "I've always wanted to meet you, whether you're glamorous or not," he wrote. "What the hell, I'm certainly not . . . you are not alone, as far as I'm concerned. And you have pleased me much, and probably displeased me much, too, like a wife; but do you want it any different from that? That means the relationship has some vitality to it."[59]

His qualified enthusiasm for Harper's poetry had faded. In a "Carol darling" letter, he said she had "seemed to indulge . . . in what is one of your grave faults as a writer—the flying off in many directions at once."

In a more personal vein, he wrote, "I think, darling Carol, you are darling to many men. I think that they think of you as Woman, as Eve, if you will . . . So you are impinged upon by the attitudes and needs of differing men. All right, these impingements grew under the conditions you lived in (in) Seattle. They merely reinforced your natural vice."[60]

This erotic, and occasionally jealous, tone had been growing steadily. Four days before Valentine's Day in 1958, Alan wrote, "I think we could love, yes, for a while. I hope we shall have the chance, but lord knows that the chance is doubtful . . . When shall we philander together? Odd, how persistent it is." Carol replied, "As for philandering, you don't really want to. Nor do I . . . I couldn't philander with anyone." Elsewhere, at about the same time, Carol, who was unsuccessfully seeking a divorce, acknowledged "various love affairs (dammit)!"[61]

Carol Harper may have been right that Alan didn't really want any philandering. His relationship with her showed signs of a man attempting to form an intimate attachment to a woman but held back by the same shyness that made him unsuccessful with girls in high school. It is not at all clear how far his sexual overtures went. His movements bore a curious similarity to those of Vridar Hunter, his friend Vardis's fictional image of himself, who dashes to a store where he believes he will find a girl he has long fancied, then hesitates to go in, goes in only when he has decided she must have left, and then is unable to speak when he finds she is still there.[62]

On a visit from Denver to Pullman, Washington, for a writers' conference early in November 1966, there was a curious meeting with such a woman. At dinner and again in the cocktail lounge, Alan told the woman he would like to see her later in the evening. By her account and others, they met at her room and then drove downtown for a second dinner and drinks. After the bar closed, they talked about his publishing and her dissertation plans. "His emotional hunger for non-demanding companionship was apparent to me," the woman wrote years later. The evening was apparently a long one. "His sense of propriety won with the dawning day, and he reluctantly left me," she wrote. This was about five-thirty AM. A few days later the woman got a letter from Alan saying that she "certainly quickly became dear to me" and speaking of their "childish fumbling." He urged her to write to him at a separate post office box that he maintained so he could receive mail without Mae or Karen seeing it. The woman was not to use his name but address the envelope to Southwestern Publishing Associates. He addressed her as "Dear One."[63]

Certainly Mae Swallow had reason for jealousy, even if she did not know of such subterfuges as Alan's secret post office box. She must have known that she did not provide her husband with the kind of intellectual companionship he might have craved, and that he had ample opportunity to seek the attentions of other women who shared his interests.

Understandably, strains developed in the Swallow marriage. "It was painful," Karen Swallow recalled. "My father was very shy as a young man, and then all of a sudden his profession brought really remarkable women his way. They were literary people he corresponded with, and then a couple of them probably turned into affairs."[64]

Although during his months in bed he had aimed to cut back his commitments for 1964 by 10 percent or so, Alan published 11 of the 250 poetry manuscripts he read that year. Total production reached what he acknowledged "may be the stupid level of fifty books," with about the same figure anticipated for 1965. By 1966, he felt that he probably had "been successful in increasing problems rather than decreasing them." A staphylococcus infection had put him on antibiotics, painkillers, and crutches. To ease his burden, he hired a student for a two-year apprenticeship, with the understanding that the lad would learn the business and probably buy into it. "But," Alan said, "I am not getting out of the publishing business as yet, and probably not for a long time; even when he comes in, if he does, it would be for only part share until I quit or die or something."[65]

Looking back on his publishing career, Alan found himself "amazed that it has worked, although there is no big money involved."[66] The apprentice did much of the work on Seattle poet Eve Triem's *Poems,* published under the imprint Poetry and Prose Editions, but in Vi Gale's judgment the arrangement did not work well.[67] Alan let the apprentice go in June 1964.[68] By the fall of 1965, he had a new assistant but found that "the boy and the shipping have become more worrisome" and he would have to do more of the work himself.[69] When the boy showed up for only an hour and failed to return as promised, Alan engaged a new one.[70] The new helper was apparently not much better but by June 1966 Alan thought the shipping situation was "settling down a little bit, as the boy is out of school and has more time and perhaps can learn more about the stock."[71] A month later, he abandoned having the shipping done in-house.[72]

Alan was soon able to start driving again, with part of his leg in a cast. He told Carol he hoped to throw away the crutches any day. He also apologized that his disability prevented him from getting very often to the secret post office box. He said arrangements for the box had been made with the help of his mother, visiting from Fort Collins. She, he said, had "helped me arrange these matters a bit after the blow-up." Long-simmering marital problems had apparently come to a head in the Swallow household. Alan took Carol's letters home, hid them among his papers, and answered them late at night, when Mae was asleep. "Yes, it is dangerous, but if I am careful, will work," he assured Carol. Once he told her he was writing fast because "I have little time alone." In one of these late-night missives, he wrote, "this quick, quick note, scratched indeed, is to let you know that I am still with you."[73]

Karen was looking around for a college, concentrating on those in New England and the Pacific Northwest, where she could ski. Her thoughts and her life changed when her father took her to buy a winter coat, and the sales clerk recommended Lewis and Clark College in Portland. She was intrigued, and Alan wrote to Vi Gale asking what kind of a school it was. "He was very anxious that she find a good school to go to," Gale recalled. After checking schools out, he and Mae favored the one in Portland, although Karen was still flirting with New England, where she applied to four schools. Lewis and Clark was finally chosen, in a kind of package deal providing for Alan to lecture there when he visited.[74] Karen's parents drove to Portland to help her settle in, stopping for Alan to give a lecture in Idaho on the way.[75]

As a student at Lewis and Clark, Karen made trips abroad under the auspices of the American Friends Service Committee. On one she took part in the last Aldermaston peace march, a three-day outing from the village of Aldermaston to London. The president at Lewis and Clark objected to Karen's participation and attempted to have her brought home, but her father objected that the march was not anti-British. He said that as an ACLU officer he would gladly sue to protect her right to participate. Karen completed the march. She also went to Mexico, serving in a village with no electricity, and to Yugoslavia in a group of twenty-two for four months.[76]

On November 29, 1965, Karen, due to graduate in a month from Lewis and Clark, was married to William Pressly of Portland, the son of a Presbyterian minister. Mae, worried about Alan's driving when he was exhausted, wanted to fly to Portland for the wedding, but Alan wanted to take the Jaguar because driving was "one of the few pleasures I have left, outside my work."[77] He gave in, and they flew.[78] After the wedding Gale gave a "rip roaring" party for the Swallows. Guests included poet William Stafford, novelist Mary Barnard, and other writers from as far away as Seattle and Corvallis, Oregon. "When I really think of a bomb that dropped on the house, it would have knocked out all the Northwest literary life," Gale said.[79]

The world of typography was turning from hot lead to offset, a process in which photographic plates are prepared for printing. Just before his coronary, Alan rented a small press with the idea of establishing a small production shop in Taos. The plan fell through, and the shop was successively subleased to three printers who ran it part time for Swallow work. For larger-scale production, Alan contracted with World Press of Denver, but World was letterpress, not offset, so he partnered with the company to buy a medium-size offset press and camera. He still had the handpress he had purchased with borrowed money in 1939. For him it was a keepsake, but he loaned it to friends who used it.[80]

Alan remained on anticholesterol and anticoagulant drugs, and wrote to his authors that he understood there might be some concern about his heart because of his "work load and incessant hours." Visiting him at this time, Vardis Fisher was surprised to find that his friend Alan had gone completely gray. "We worried a good bit about it because we loved Alan and were aware that he was pushing himself too hard," said Opal.[81] Alan promised to cut back on titles for 1966, knowing that this would happen whatever he did, because of shipping problems. He had given up on the apprenticeship, and hired boys to do the shipping. Two were excellent, others were not, so he often had to throw his crutches aside and do the work himself. He felt his work as editor was suffering, and he was unable to plan as many projects as usual. Besides, he thought his obligations to authors made cutting back not as easy as it sounded. He vowed to turn down offers to buy part or all of his operations "merely to exploit them for a return." The business continued to venture into new fields, including a contract with the Xerox Corporation to produce and sell enlarged copies of Sage Books at a 5 percent royalty.[82]

The Swallows saw 1966 in with a loud and boisterous party at the Fishers' house in Idaho. When they arrived home, Mae was coming down with the flu. She still went to work at the university, but was unable to help Alan with the accumulated "mountain of mail."[83] Alan's wife was unhappy with her job and talked of quitting, but felt she could not afford it.[84] Her husband, who was on a new antibiotic, felt his leg was holding up well and hoped to avoid further surgery. Still, there was the pain. To his friend Mark Harris, he wrote that he had found a new drug, the blood-thinning medicine Coumadin, that he believed would make a difference. "I think I'll make it through tonight all right, and then be okay," he said. He was gauging the outlook day by day.[85]

Harry Chrisman, hearing of all this in letters from Alan Swallow to "authors and friends," felt Alan "stretching out a hand—perhaps subconsciously—for help." Chrisman himself, unhappy with a newspaper job, had simply quit and moved to Denver. It had worked out wonderfully for him and his wife, he said. It was, he told Alan, better to quit sometimes that to "ruin one's self." As an alternative, he suggested, maybe Alan should create a separate shipping department, freeing him to concentrate on editing and production. Chrisman conceded that this was probably not practical, but "I can see that you are stretched too fine for your own good . . . so you will have to make that decision to ease yourself out of that bear trap someway."[86]

In the mid-1960s, Alan tried abandoning his no-salesman policy, employing some on a commission basis to handle paperbacks, "very choosy to be of any value to the books."[87] He was not happy with the salesmen. The one he contacted in New York wrote him that he didn't think his help would be of any value. "The one in the South," he complained, "never did anything and then retired." The one in New England said the Swallow books were too esoteric. This left him with one in the West and two in the Midwest, "right in there trying," but not worth the extra expense.[88] Alan made a number of changes in his publishing business during the summer of 1966 in an effort to get it more manageable. The business had, he said, "outgrown my particular methods, yet I am constitutionally opposed to creating an organization."[89]

As a poet, Alan continued to adhere to traditional forms. He urged poets to avoid the increasingly popular slant, or approximate, rhymes in favor of full rhymes. Yet as a critic, he was open to experimental work, saying it "has netted us some very fine poems undoubtedly several great poems—which are of the sort that investigate one corner of our experience with great ability." When publishing first books of poetry, he refused to have introductions to them written, saying, "the poet's work must sail forth on its own." On November 22, 1966, he wrote that poetry readings were getting far more attention than they deserved and he did not think they would significantly enhance a poet's reputation. Illustrations of poetic works he described as a "bastard art." In other words, neither platform appearances nor pictures were as important as the poet's words on the page. James Schevill aptly called Swallow "an idealist of the word."[90]

In October 1966 Vardis and Opal were visiting with the Swallows in the yard of their York Street home and "saw with violent intensity" that Alan "had a wife on his neck" and possibly "the other woman making demands upon him that he couldn't honorably meet." Looking back later, Vardis wrote, "Poor sad friend! Poor dear sad tragic Alan."[91] As Vardis told the story, Virginia McConnell stopped by in the afternoon to talk with Alan about a manuscript she was editing for him. When Vardis got into a discussion of literary style with McConnell, Alan interrupted and told him to "stop trying to lead her around by the nose." Mae fled in fury into the house.[92] To Vardis, she seemed close to mental collapse.

Rumors had been going around that Alan was having affairs, and Mae had the reputation of being a jealous woman. There was talk that she was drinking heavily.[93]

When Frank Waters next visited, Mae asked him, "Frank, what'll I do? . . . I've been Alan's wife for more than twenty years."[94] The Fishers had told her before that they saw no reason for her jealousy; by this time, they were not so sure. "Opal and I were made innocent victims in regard to a certain Swallow relationship and Mae I am sure had the idea that Opal and I were in league against her," Vardis wrote. "We were not."[95]

More cracks were showing in the marriage about which, when they were a young wartime couple, Alan Swallow had written so movingly:

Each night in public stations
Sit those more lonely than the homeless,
And, rising to embrace,
Kiss frightened lips
And inadvertent tears.

And thus were we. I rose
To follow after—
To think: at eight o'clock
She left Denver, at twelve,
Cheyenne.

   What are those places,
Those towns we shuttle through?
They are not ever known
Except as names where I
Would touch your reaching hand.[96]

More than twenty years after these wartime partings, the reaching and touching were less evident. Alan apparently told Vardis he had tried to get Mae to see a psychiatrist. "It now seems likely," Vardis wrote, "that he was the one who needed a psychiatrist, but felt disgust and contempt for them."[97]

On Memorial Day weekend in 1966, Alan took Mae on a flying trip to Portland for a visit with Karen and Bill, and described it as an anniversary present for his wife. They had been married thirty years. Later in the fall, Alan paid what would be his last visit to Powell, where he appeared to the family to be in good spirits.[98]

In a vine-covered study in the backyard of his California home, Yvor Winters spent much of that summer working on the overdue manuscript of his critical book *Forms of Discovery* for the Swallow press. "It is a very quiet place; I felt as if Alan were watching me," he reflected.[99]

Carol Harper sent Alan the manuscript of her book-length poem about the Big Bend of the Columbia River, where she had lived so long and gone through so many tribulations. "I tend to like this work pretty well," he said, although he did not think Harper wrote as well as she had.[100] A few days before Thanksgiving, the two had one of their rare telephone conversations. Carol said she called him about a book of poems he was publishing, written by her merchant seaman protégé Bob Rawls. As she recalled, Alan asked her, "How are you, Carol?" and she failed to realize "his own fragility."[101]

That fragility apparently made him unaccustomedly careless in business matters. In an invoice he sent to Caroline Bancroft, a gossipy Denver writer of popular historical booklets, on November 22, she found three errors, one on consigned stock that was in her favor and one on a payment account that was in his.[102]

As always, Alan Swallow kept busy. He was publishing a new novel by Frank Waters, *The Woman at Otowi Crossing*. On November 16, he guided the author on a round of talks to the Pikes Peak Historical Society, the University of Colorado Center, and the Colorado Council of the Arts and Humanities, and then joined him in an appearance on the Bill Barker show on Denver's broadcast station KOA. The next day they made the rounds again, for *Denver Post* and *Rocky Mountain News* interviews and visits to bookstores. Waters noted that his publisher's face was unusually flushed.[103]

November 23 was another typical workday. Alan mailed a postcard to Winters saying he was about to send him the last of the galley sheets for the still unfinished critical book.[104] In the evening he attended a meeting of Westerners, a Denver club. A fellow member, a bookseller, asked him if Waters's nonfiction *Midas of the Rockies* would continue to be available.[105] Alan felt tired and left early at eight-thirty.[106]

The next morning, on Thanksgiving Day, Mae Swallow woke to the humming of her husband's electric typewriter. Approaching his workroom, she found him seated in his chair with his head slumped over a table. Alan Swallow was dead at the age of fifty-one.[107] A partial manuscript of Carol Harper's *Big Bend* was in the collating machine on the heavy black desk on the north porch of the Swallows' house.[108] At her home in Seattle, Harper was busy retyping the last ten pages.[109]

In a telephone conversation the day before, Alan had asked his daughter once again if she would take the business over when he was gone. Again she found herself unfitted for the task. "It created a great deal of sadness for Dad as well as for me," Karen Swallow said. "We both let each other down."[110]

10

Postmortem

Mae called her mother in Powell as the Elders were getting ready to go out to a family Thanksgiving dinner. At two PM her father, Ralph Elder, sat down and wrote to her in his meticulous longhand that Alan "evidently went the way he would have wished to (at work)." He added his confidence that Mae had "the ability and poise to meet the situation and carry on as Allan [sic] would have wished to do." He also said he was certain that Alan would not "leave his business affairs in a mess (as they say) and as some people do."[1]

In Portland, Vi Gale was getting ready to leave the house for lunch with a writer friend when she heard a radio broadcaster say something about Alan Swallow in Denver and an apparent heart attack. She called a man she knew who worked for the *Portland Oregonian* and he said he would check the Associated Press wire. When her friend came back to the phone, he said, "The news is bad; he's gone." Gale felt that she had known it all along.[2]

At his breakfast table on Friday morning, the poet and journalist Thomas Hornsby Ferril opened his *Rocky Mountain News* and read of his friend's death. A few minutes later, he opened the family mailbox, found a Sage Books catalog for 1965 on top of the pile, and counted the titles. There were 209, new and old. "Alan Swallow's name must be perpetuated by some fitting memorial," he wrote in his column the next week.[3] The University of Denver announced plans for an Alan Swallow Memorial Fund.[4]

When he received a copy of a circular letter from Dean John R. Little of the university faculty asking for donations to the fund, Vardis Fisher wrote that he favored the idea, but considered Swallow both "a great man in some ways" and "a sly and calculating deceiver" and believed that "all should be known about him, the great and the not so great, the admirable and the detestable." "Damn it, I loved Alan, but he put me in such an impossible position that the resentment still flows through my nerves," he told a friend.[5] To another he said, "You're jumping the gun: let's not have a minor 'John F. Kennedy' apotheosis on Alan. If there is to be any kind of memorial . . . let it be considered and unanimous."[6] In the spring of 1968, the poet Rolfe Humphries donated money to finance a scholarship in the Swallow name, covering fee, tuition, board and room, and some travel over at least a four-year period.[7]

Two days after Alan Swallow's death, a memorial service was held in the newly rebuilt Gothic-style Evans Chapel at the university, with an Episcopal priest presiding. Swallow was not a religious man, but his daughter was a religious woman, and it was Karen who pushed for the church service.[8] A selection of her father's poems was read, including the one he chose to open his volume *The Remembered Land:*

Stone

The older poets were wrong, speaking the lone
Imperturbable, imperishable, imponderable stone
Because a rock faced sun surviving human eyes.
For even stone dissolves and dies.
With wear of water, split of frost,
Stones break, and down the river-sewers are lost.

And feeble too those men who placed
A stone at the grave's end, now with the words
    effaced.

Who knows the hawk speaks well of rock and cliff,
Finding a haven there when wings are stiff.
And man in his hawk-days breathed life in stone,
Chipping and grinding it down, extending his bone.
Turn hammer words on rock, the fugitive:
So stone will live.

The family requested contributions to the ACLU in lieu of flowers.[9] Alan Swallow was cremated, as he had wished. The family wanted to scatter the ashes from an airplane, but they were told this would be illegal, and the ashes were deposited in the backyard of the York Street house. A gravestone was later placed in the cemetery in Powell.

On Sunday evening, at her home near Lake Washington in Seattle, Carol Harper had just put into the mailbox, to be sent to Alan, a page from a nautical magazine concerning her friend Rawls. Her husband, Maurice, in the kitchen, had the radio on, and heard an announcer say that Alan Swallow had died on Thanksgiving Day of a heart attack in Denver. Carol sat down and wrote a round-robin letter to her now scattered children. "I am lonely," she wrote. "As a writer, I am now lonely beyond loneliness . . . Alan has been my support—the bulwark beneath me, the solid base beneath all my efforts . . . Dammit, why couldn't he have been saved?"[10]

That same evening, she and Maurice sent a telegram to Mae expressing their condolences and those of present and former Experiment Press and *Experiment* magazine staff and contributors. They declared that "Alan's loss to the literature of the world is irreparable." The first draft of the wire contained a passage, deleted before it was sent, asking what they could do to help either personally or in the conduct of the Swallow press. "If you want us to take over some of the work for a while or permanently, to carry it on under the same name, let us know," they said. The first draft of the night letter, sent for delivery the following day, was addressed "Dear May," a misspelling of the name of a woman they had never met. The final draft was addressed "Dear Mrs. Swallow," but the words were crossed out, leaving it uncertain what the final salutation, if any, was.[11]

That same day, in Hagerman, Vardis Fisher wrote a letter to Mae outlining his relations with the Swallow publishing firm, pointing out that he had a contract for publication of a huge book on western mining camps that he and Opal had written together. Both of them, he said, had "heard Alan say a number of times that he had told you that in case of his death you were to fulfill all contracts." A participant in the negotiations about the book described them as "rather sticky." Vardis offered his advice and help if Alan's widow should wish to sell the firm to a New York publisher. "We love you, Mae, and are your devoted friends," he said. "Count on us."[12] Later, he offered to withdraw the mining camp manuscript.

Vardis soon began work on another project: a magazine article about the last weeks of Alan Swallow's life, and his death. "Whether it was a heart attack (as diagnosed) or suicide no one will probably ever know," he said. "I feel that while I can I should tell the story." Karen was reported to have said that on the fatal day her father did not take his medicine. Virginia McConnell told Vardis, "I think—I *know* that he quit." Vardis Fisher's version, if it was written, was never published.

Yvor Winters was in the midst of reading proof on *Forms of Discovery* when he received a wire from Mae with the terrible news from Denver. "Everybody said he had been working too hard for a long time," he replied. "I cannot tell you how depressed I am." As Winters expected to write an obituary essay for the *Southern Review,* he asked Mae for biographical information, including Alan's airplane and motorcycle mishaps, because "they throw a little light on the curious inner violence that contributed to his success and to his death."[13]

Denver attorney Martin Miller was retained to settle the Swallow estate and help with management of the business. On December 1 Harry Chrisman, a Denver journalist and author of western history, wrote to Miller that he had met with Alan shortly before the latter's death, to discuss a misunderstanding about a book on which he believed he was owed some money. He said Alan told him that "the laborer is worthy of his hire" and that he would send him a check for $250 "plus something extra if the book does well." Chrisman told Miller that he believed Alan would have wanted the account paid if possible. A year later Chrisman received the second of two checks for $100.[14]

Sometime after Alan's death, Carol Harper received a postcard from Alan about payments that would be due Rawls from sales of his book, and sent a copy of it to the author. She kept the original, one of the last, if not the last, of Alan's many notes and letters to writers. With the card she sent a note saying that Alan had once told her that "his wife had turned violently against me because of Alan's close working with me" and expressing uncertainty about the future of the Swallow publishing concern.[15]

On December 15, New York poet Roger Hecht, apologizing for "writing at this time about business affairs," asked about the future of his *27 Poems,* which Alan had published. He offered to pay if Mae would arrange to have the publication rights and the plates of the book transferred to him. He also sought release from an agreement giving Alan first refusal of his next book.[16]

In a letter in January, Mae and Gus Blaisdell of the University of New Mexico Press assured "friends and authors" that "for the present at least, the press will continue," although at a slower rate. All details were to be handled by Mae, Blaisdell, and Martin Miller, attorney to the estate. "No other persons have anything whatsoever to do with the press," they said. Recipients were asked to send along letters received from anyone else using the Alan Swallow letterhead.[17] Frank Waters thought it was good news that Mae was taking the lead role; Vardis Fisher did not. "She doesn't know a thing about publishing, and she has been (and is) . . . emotionally disturbed," he told Waters.[18] One of the first things Mae did under the new setup was to fire Virginia McConnell.[19] When the Fishers came to Denver on business in the spring, Mae refused to see them.[20]

Rumors began circulating about the future of the press. The University of Indiana was going to buy it. The Colorado Historical Society was interested.[21] Several wealthy Denver men were intrigued.[22] So were North Dakota State University and Wesleyan University Press.[23] Cliff's Notes also enquired about producing and marketing books on the Swallow list.[24] Most, however, wanted to buy only part of the operation. Mae wanted it to continue as one unit.[25]

On a spring day in 1967, Morton Weisman, president of the Chicago wholesale book distributor A. C. McClurg's, who was vacationing in Las Vegas, happened to be chatting with Martin Miller, who was attending a lawyers' convention. When Miller learned what Weisman did for a living, he asked to whom he thought Mae should sell the business. Weisman knew Swallow by reputation, and offered to get together a group that would buy the publishing enterprise themselves.

Back in Chicago, Weisman contacted Durett Wagner, a western historian from El Paso, Texas, then serving as dean of Kendall College in the Chicago suburb of Evanston, and Robert Rubin, a lawyer interested in scholarly books. They arranged to meet in Denver with Miller and Mae, and the business was sold in August to the Chicago concern, which operated it as Swallow Press Inc., with Wagner as its president. Mae wrote to her husband's "authors and many friends" that it had become impractical for her to continue the business alone.[26] The price was not disclosed, but Blaisdell thought Weisman had paid too much.[27] The firm operated out of a sixth-floor loft at 1139 South Wabash, south of the Chicago Loop. Half of the loft was warehouse and half office space.[28]

"No doubt you feel that a great weight has been lifted from your shoulders," a friend wrote, noting that even *Denver Post* book editor Stanton Peckham, whom Alan had thought neglected western literature, had said that "Denver's loss is Chicago's gain."[29] The sale included Sage Books and Big Mountain Press along with the Swallow name. The Chicago group acquired a backlist of about four hundred authors, and book lovers in Denver scrambled to buy up volumes before they left town.[30] "It was pretty chaotic," Gale said. "I think it was a real horror story . . . I supplied them with no less than three original manuscripts and corrected about three sets of proofs and went through all kinds of things and finally the book did come out."[31] Ada Merrill, running a bookstore in Boulder, said she had trouble getting books that she ordered from the new owners.[32]

The view from Chicago was understandably different. Van Allen Bradley, literary editor of the *Daily News,* noted "the sharply improved appearance of Swallow titles under the new ownership." The new management moved to keep in touch with Swallow writers, inviting any who would be in New York at the time of the 1968 Modern Language Association meeting to a party.[33] At the same time, Wagner was complaining that records provided by the Swallow estate were "hopelessly confused" and that the owners had inherited "previously unkept or ill-kept records" regarding the six trailer-truck loads of books that arrived from Denver.[34] Some books, the firm's lawyer said, had been "indiscriminately tossed into any carton that happened to be nearby."[35]

In any event, the Swallow family's interest in books could continue. Karen's first marriage had not lasted, and she married Jon Hagen, owner of Longfellow's Bookstore in Portland, in 1976. Their son, Nile Hagen, worked in the antiquarian book outlet.

Wagner's accounting said the Swallow press had eight thousand Vardis Fisher books, including sixty-eight copies of *Orphans in Gethsemane*.[36] Fisher said he paid $4,000 for one thousand copies of *Orphans*. He also paid $1,000 for five hundred copies of another book, but the accounting showed there were none. "Apparently Swallow printed none for me," he said.[37] Vardis told Frederick Manfred that Wagner's letter had thrown him into a mild state of shock. "To put it briefly," he said, "unless there are books of mine by the thousands in the . . . warehouse, Alan deceived and defrauded me of thousands of dollars." Earlier Fisher had said, "Alan and I were not much to draw contracts."[38] Since then, he said, he had amassed conclusive evidence that Swallow's "bookkeeping was dreadful." In the end, he said he was resigned to losing about $1,200 but would "not press any claim against a wonderful guy, over his head financially, and apparently over his head with a woman."

John Milton, who had sparred with Swallow on literary issues as a colleague at the University of Denver, found Swallow "a strange man, helping the worthy western writers almost to the extent of obsession, and then at the same time being so utterly stupid on many literary matters."[39] Milton also said that he found his "ambivalent feelings toward Alan are shared by many, many people, including those who knew him best."

Frederick Manfred, for instance, wrote to Frank Waters, "I think Alan did us much good. But at the same time I think he did too much business on his cuffs instead of on business sheets."[40] This left his widow with financial problems. The purchase price from the new owners was to be paid over a fifteen-year period. The government was planning to audit Alan's income tax returns for the last six years, including a questionable $12,000 business loss he claimed in 1965.[41] To the Fishers it seemed "more probable . . . that he was utterly fed up and couldn't see his way out of the mess and simply quit." On a visit to Boise in the fall of 1967, Durett Wagner gave Vardis the impression "that the Press has good grounds against the Estate."[42]

Milton said Mae "very likely was the victim of Alan's escapades and mistakes."[43] Shortly after Swallow's death, Vardis Fisher typed his "impressions of his relationship with McConnell." He said McConnell had written him a long and "very revealing" letter quoting from Alan's letters to her. "It is strongly my impression that he was in over his head financially and with McConnell," Vardis said. In his view, Mae was an ignorant woman who cared nothing about books, was embarrassed in literary gatherings because she did not understand what was being said, and "was the worst possible wife for Alan . . . but neither was Virginia the woman for him."

Years later McConnell, by then Virginia McConnell Simmons, was asked by Colorado magazine editor Thomas M. Auer, then beginning work on a projected biography of Alan Swallow, whether she had an affair with the proposed book's subject. She declined to answer and chastised him for concentrating on trivial matters. In 2007 the author of this book asked Simmons the same questions and again she declined to respond to them.[44] Vardis Fisher's view of Virginia McConnell was that she was a good writer and editor, but emotionally childlike. "After Alan's daughter got married, his house was empty," Fisher said.[45]

Some of Alan Swallow's authors were increasingly unhappy. Caroline Bancroft accused Mae of "welching" on payments due to her but did not blame Mae as much as her husband. "Alan was the dishonest one, always borrowing from Peter to pay Paul and juggling figures," she said.[46]

Vardis Fisher wrote Mae three times about a manuscript and photographs for the book about mining camps that he had submitted to Alan, but received no reply. Arguing that his earnings were so meager he was "eligible for [President Lyndon B.] Johnson's poverty program," Fisher pressed the Swallow estate for overdue royalty payments.[47]

"The Swallow Press should have remained in Denver, but there was no individual with the money to finance it or editorial brains to carry on his idea of small first editions followed by reprints done in low-cost offsets," Harry Chrisman said.[48] The first book from the new ownership was *Forms of Discovery,* a collection of critical essays by Yvor Winters, followed by *Pumpkin Seed,* Frank Waters's account of life among the Hopi Indians, and *The Pit and Other Poems* by Lucien Stryke. Such regional favorites as *Guide to Colorado Ghost Towns and Mining Camps* and *Newport in the Rockies,* Waters's history of Colorado Springs, also appeared in new dress.[49]

On November 9 Wagner came to Denver to address the Colorado Authors League, and felt that he was "over defensive and gave the appearance of unsureness" as an interloper talking to admirers of the real Alan Swallow in his own hometown. One person in the audience said Wagner seemed "overwhelmed with what needs to be done."[50]

Weisman told Tom McGrath the newly constituted firm would be able to "provide a much more broadly based and aggressive promotional activity" than Swallow had. McGrath submitted a manuscript but said he was terrified of "long silences" from the editors.[51] McConnell obtained release from an agreement she had made with Alan giving the press first option on her next book, after indicating she might sue if her request was not granted. Her attitude toward the new owners, she said, had become "thoroughly negative."[52]

Vardis Fisher was "strongly of the impression that the Swallow Press, having made an inventory of what it bought, is not at all happy."[53] Although the agreement had been that all business correspondence would be transferred to the new owners, and Mae would keep only personal letters to Alan, Wagner learned early in 1970 that a number of business files remained in Denver. Particularly disturbing was the discovery of a file concerning the agreement with Harcourt, Brace for joint publication of the Anaïs Nin diaries. Harcourt was contending that it had withdrawn from the agreement after publication of the second volume of the work. When Mae Swallow's files were searched, a two-page agreement was found providing for joint publication of all four volumes. "We were screwed by Harcourt because we couldn't support our case (whereas all that time the documentation was lying buried in the files . . .)," Wagner said.[54]

In 1973 Weisman worked out a deal to transfer the press to a holding corporation, Brent, Kutner, Weisman Inc.[55] When a writer asked him in 1977 whether the firm was in financial trouble, he said it always had been, although 1976 had been its best year in sales. "It is in the nature of small publishers to have financial difficulties," Weisman said.[56] On June 19, 1979, Swallow Press was acquired by Ohio University Press under a joint imprint agreement to be reviewed every ten years.[57]

Among the last books published by Alan Swallow in his lifetime were *27 Poems* by Roger Hecht and *My Father Spoke of His Riches,* a book of poems by Natalie S. Robins. They illustrate the catholicity of taste that guided his publishing. Hecht, as poet and reviewer Barbara Guest observed in the *New York Times Book Review,* is "skilled, precise and controlled," at times echoing the seventeenth-century poets Swallow admired. Robins is a much more impulsive and emotional poet who Guest said could profit from some of Hecht's graceful precision.

Alan Swallow had published some of America's outstanding authors. He had pioneered publishing in the West. His Sage Books brought to light nuggets of western history that might well have been forgotten. The thirty-five titles in his New Poetry Series brought forth works by emerging poets from the West and elsewhere. At the time of his death, tributes flowed in from writers he had published and befriended. "One could disagree with him," one such message said, "but one had always to respect his judgment and integrity."[58] On the other hand, when one writer working on an obituary notice telephoned *Author and Publisher* seeking comment, nobody there remembered that somebody named Swallow had once been the magazine's editor.[59]

Alan Swallow's life was one of triumph and torment, of achievement and anguish. His daughter believed the greatest gift he gave her was "the unquestioning inner strength and freedom to stand apart from any group; to be an individual and to go against the established grain when necessary."[60]

An equally perceptive and sadder comment came from Swallow's old high school and college friend Ross Jamieson, who had made a successful career in business after leaving the University of Wyoming and returning to Powell. Alan, Jamieson said, "was possibly a quiet rebel who challenged the conservative wisdom of the day." However, he added, "I always thought that he did not get enough fun out of life."[61]

It is perhaps idle, but nonetheless tempting, to speculate how Swallow's life and career might have changed had he moved, when he had the chance, to the East, which has remained the heart of U.S. publishing. Surely he would have had more opportunity than his modest York Street home provided to mingle comfortably with a greater number of notable writers. When Swallow made his first, tentative moves as a Denver publisher in 1946, the city's population by the latest count was a little over 320,000. By 2010, Denver was the heart of a metropolitan statistical area that was home to more than 2.5 million people. Despite these demographic changes, the front range of the Rocky Mountains, which a boy who dreamed of being a publisher gazed at from the sagebrush flats of Powell, Wyoming, remained remote from the steely canyons of Manhattan. Alan Swallow, though, had done his bit to diminish the distance.

NOTES

BIBLIOGRAPHY

INDEX

Notes

Note: Because of Tom Auer's untimely death and the fact that I received many of the cited documents, such as letters and transcripts of his interviews, in banker boxes (see Marilyn Auer's foreword), the citations in many of the notes are of necessity incomplete. Arrangements are being considered to donate these materials, currently lent to me from a private collection, to an archive so that they will be available to future scholars. In the meantime, the following locations contain pertinent documents:

Bird Library, Syracuse University: Alan Swallow papers.
Center for Southwest Research, University of New Mexico: Frank Waters correspondence.
Homesteaders Museum, Powell, Wyoming: Land transaction records.
Special Collections Department, Boise State University: Vardis Fisher correspondence.
Stanford University Library: Yvor Winters and Janet Lewis correspondence and Alan Swallow's correspondence with them.
Western Kentucky University: Robert Penn Warren papers.
University of Illinois at Chicago, Richard J. Daley Library: Swallow Press archives.
University of North Dakota, Chester Fritz Library: Thomas McGrath correspondence.

ABBREVIATIONS

AS   Alan Swallow
CH   Carol Harper
FW   Frank Waters
KS   Karen Swallow
MS   Mae Swallow
NMQR   *New Mexico Quarterly Review*
RPW   Robert Penn Warren
TA   Thomas M. Auer
VF   Vardis Fisher
YW   Yvor Winters

I: A BOOKISH YOUNGSTER

1. Vera Cowel, interview by Thomas M. Auer, Fort Collins, CO, 2; Sharon K. Chickering, "Great Escapes, Leadville," *Denver Post,* Aug. 3, 1997, 9–19; T. A. Larson, *History of Wyoming* (Lincoln: Univ. of Nebraska Press, 1965), 173–74.

2. Vera Cowel to TA, Mar. 5, 1991.

3. Art Eldridge to Vera Cowel, undated.

4. Marcia Meredith Hensley, *Staking Her Claim: Women Homesteading the West* (Glendo, WY: High Plains Press, 2008), 11, 36–37.

5. Cowel interview, 3.

6. "Certificate of Filing Water Right Application," June 23, 1910.

7. "Certificate. Homestead," May 8, 1917.

8. "Notice of Intention to Make Proof," Mar. 5, 1918.

9. "Plenty of Water for Fields but Drinking Water Is Scarce," *Powell Tribune,* June 14–20, year unclear.

10. Robert Koelling, *First National Bank of Powell: The History of a Bank, a Community, and a Family* (Powell, WY: First National Bank of Powell, 1997), 12.

11. Jane Johnstone, "From Saltsage to Security: A Settlement Is Born, Takes Root and Grows to Become a Thriving Wyoming Community," in *Powell: 1909–1959* (Powell, WY: First National Bank of Powell, 1959), 13.

12. Alta Helen Myers Swallow to Shirley Walters, undated; "Death Calls Edgar A. Swallow, Powell Farmer and Business Man," *Powell Tribune,* Apr. 27, 1948.

13. "Report of Alan Swallow," Powell Public Schools, Powell, WY, Spring 1925.

14. Cowel interview, 3–4; Ross A. Jamieson to TA, Mar. 25, 1996.

15. "Homesteading at Powell, Wyoming," memo to TA, undated.

16. Ross A. Jamieson to TA, Mar. 25, 1996; Cowel interview, 27.

17. Martha A. Hume, "A Big Man Goes Down," *Small Press Review,* Spring 1997, 7; clippings in family collection.

18. Alan Swallow, *Two Stories* (Denver: Alan Swallow, Publisher, 1953), 5.

19. Alan Swallow, "Short Haul to Bookstore for Modern Day Readers," newspaper clipping, June 23, 1957.

20. Kenneth Donald McCracken, "E. Haldeman-Julius: A Critical Evaluation" (master's thesis, Kansas State Teachers College, May 1956), 1–2.

21. William F. Ryan, "In Search of Haldeman-Julius," *American Rationalist,* Sept.–Oct. 1973; Gene DeGuuson, "E. Haldeman-Julius" (unpublished speech text, Tri-State Craftsmen's Club, May 6, 1991).

22. McCracken, "E. Haldeman-Julius," 30–32, 37–38.

23. Mark Scott, "The Little Blue Books in the War on Bigotry and Bunk," *Kansas History,* Autumn 1978, 155.

24. AS, under the pseudonym "e. cummings e.," "Derelict," in *Sage: A Literary Journal,* Oct. 1933, 9–10; AS, "The Tramp" (photocopy, unidentified publication, Fall 1940).

25. Jamieson to TA, Mar. 25, 1996; "Record of Swallow, Alan," Powell High School, 1929; Cowel interview.

26. Jamieson to TA, Mar. 25, 1996; Cowel interview, 12; Cowel to TA, Mar. 5, 1991; MS, interview by TA, Sept. 26, 1987; Swallow, *Two Stories,* 7–14; Hume, "A Big Man Goes Down," 7.

27. Jamieson to TA, Mar. 25, 1996.

28. Cowel interview, 13–14.

29. AS, "Salutatory Speech on Commencement Day," May 20, 1932 (handwritten text by speaker, Univ. of Wyoming "Honor Scholarship," Apr. 27, 1932).

30. Cowel interview.

31. Alan Swallow, undated handwritten note.

2: BIG MAN ON CAMPUS

1. Alan Swallow, "A Freshman Looks at College" and "The Story of a Green Freshman" (unpublished essays, Fall 1932).

2. Herb Harmatz, "Alan Swallow Has Printer's Ink in Blood; Sets by Hand," Louisiana State University publication, May 16, 1940; Alan Swallow, "The Careful Young Men," *The Nation,* Mar. 9, 1957, 209.

3. "Statistical Review" and advertisement, *Polk City Directory,* 1931–32.

4. Ross Jamieson to TA, Mar. 15, 1996; *Laramie, WY, City Directory,* 1934–35.

5. Cora Sliger to Alta Swallow, June 19, 1933; *City Directory,* 1934–35; Swallow, "Jottings" (handwritten manuscript, Jan. 26, 1933).

6. Upton Sinclair to AS, Oct. 4, 1932; Stanley Burnshaw to AS, Jan. 25, 1935.

7. AS, "Jottings," Feb. 11, 1933.

8. AS, "Jottings," Jan. 18, Feb. 13, Feb. 22, Mar. 2, 1933.

9. "Powell Young Man Helps in Publication of Literary Magazine," "University Group Issues Magazine" (undated clippings from *Branding Iron*); Editorials, *Sage,* Oct. 1933, and Spring 1966, 4.

10. Edgar Swallow Jr. to AS, Nov. 10, 1933; Cowel interview; AS, "Dearly Beloved," *Wyoming Student Verse: 1927–1937.*

11. Ted Olson to AS, Feb. 17, 1934.

12. Mae Swallow, interview by TA, Sept. 26, 1987.

13. Mary Seik to AS, Jan. 5, 1934.

14. "Regionalism," and AS, "Hart Crane: A Second Quest," both in *Sage,* Jan. 1934; "Second Issue of 'Sage' Appears This Week," *Branding Iron* (undated clipping); AS, "Story of a Publisher," *New Mexico Quarterly,* Winter 1966–67, 302.

15. AS, "Poem," *Sage,* Feb. 1934; Editorials, *Sage,* Feb. and Mar. 1934; AS, "Story of a Publisher," 302–3.

16. AS, ed., "A New Poetry: An Anthology, 1934–37" (unpublished).

17. MS interview.

18. MS interview; Cowel interview; AS, *College Verse,* Apr. 1937; AS, "Alan Swallow Writes," *Sage,* Spring 1966, 3–4; AS to Dick Elman, Dec. 22, 1960.

19. *Laramie Directory,* 1937.

20. "Utah Debate Team Meets Local Men," *Branding Iron* (undated clipping).

21. "Bob White to Edit Quill Magazine This Year," and "Eight Elected to Quill Membership," *Branding Iron* (undated clippings).

22. "Cosmopolitan Club to Subscribe for Journal," and "Skalds Elects Officers," *Branding Iron* (undated clippings).

23. AS, "Weed-Smoke," *Wyoming Student Verse.*

24. AS, "Rainbow: Three Sonnets to Hart Crane," *The Parchment,* Nov. 1934; Wilson Clough, "Alan Swallow as Poet" (unpublished manuscript, undated).

25. AS, "The Open Range," and Anonymous, "Writers Drop Sex for Social Topics," *Branding Iron* (undated clippings).

26. AS, "The Open Range," and Anonymous, "Challenge Sent Out for Debate on U.W. R.O.T.C.," *Branding Iron* (undated clippings).

27. Arthur T. Coumbe and Lee S. Harford, *U.S. Army Cadet Command: The 10-Year History* (Fort Monroe, VA: Office of the Command Historian, U.S. Army Cadet Command, 1996); Joseph Sestak, interview by author, Laramie, WY, Sept. 30, 2005.

28. Program, 47th annual commencement of the University of Wyoming, June 8, 1937.

29. Mae Swallow interview; Cowel interview.

30. " . . . among College Poets," *Branding Iron* (undated clipping); "Richard Elman, A Publisher for Poets," *Saturday Review,* July 22, 1961, 33.

31. Karen Swallow, interview by TA, Portland, OR, Jan. 1988.

3: DOWN ALTITUDES OF AIR

1. Joseph Blotner, *Robert Penn Warren: A Biography* (New York: Random House, 1997), 105; Yvor Winters, *The Function of Criticism: Problems and Exercises* (Denver, CO: Alan Swallow, 1957), 22; Robert Penn Warren, "The Briar Patch," in *I'll Take My Stand: The South and the Agrarian Tradition,* by Twelve Southerners (New York: Peter Smith, 1951), 253–54.

2. Donald Davidson, "A Mirror for Artists," 29; John Crowe Ransom, "Reconstructed but Unregenerate," 7–8; Allen Tate, "Remarks on the Southern Religion," 157; Andrew Nelson Lytle, "The Hind Tit," 205–6, all in Twelve Southerners, *I'll Take My Stand,* 42.

3. MS interview; AS to Harry Chrisman, July 25, 1961.

4. AS, *The Nameless Sight: Poems 1937–1956* (Denver: Swallow Paperbooks, 1956), 16; Alice Moser to AS, undated.

5. MS interview; Blotner, *Robert Penn Warren,* 113; KS interview by TA; AS, "The Mavericks," *Critique: Studies in Modern Fiction,* Winter 1959, 75.

6. Cutrer, *Parnassus on the Mississippi,* 1–5, 24–36.

7. MS interview; Cutrer, *Parnassus,* 48–49; "LSU Resumes Publication of Its Distinguished Literary Journal," *LSU Outlook,* Jan. 1965, 1–5.

8. MS interview; Cutrer, *Parnassus,* 63, 83, 84; Albert Joseph Montesi, "*The Southern Review* (1935–1942): A History and Evaluation" (dissertation, Pennsylvania State Univ., Aug. 1955); Jean Stafford, "Some Letters to Peter and Eleanor Taylor," *Shenandoah,* Spring 1979, 27.

9. MS interview.

10. H. S. Merriam to AS, July 19, 1937.

11. Gretchen Kabel, grade transcript, Louisiana State University and A&M College, Mar. 10, 1954.

12. MS interview; Blotner, *Robert Penn Warren,* 66.

13. AS, "On Reading and Writing," *Sunday Denver Post,* Jan. 20, 1957.

14. Cutrer, *Parnassus,* 36.

15. Robert Penn Warren, *New and Selected Essays* (New York: Random House, 1989), 24.

16. William F. Claire, ed., *Publishing in the West: Alan Swallow, Some Letters and Commentaries* (Santa Fe: The Lightning Tree, 1974), 24.

17. Cleanth Brooks to TA, May 29, 1990; Cleanth Brooks, interview in *Southern Reader: A Preview of Current Books on Southern History and Culture,* Summer 1989.

18. Ann Winslow to AS, Sept. 28, 1937; Ray B. West to AS, Sept. 27, 1937; Alice Moser to AS, undated.

19. AS, *A Ballad Concerning a Monk Who Fell in the Moat* (privately printed, Nov. 1937).

20. Daniel Harrison to AS, Jan. 5, 1938.

21. MS interview; Ted Olson to AS, Jan. 5, 1939.

22. Koelling, *First National Bank of Powell,* 62–74; Jerred Metz, *The Last Eleven Days of Earl Durand* (Glendo, WY: High Plains Press, 2005), 22, 26, 34, 148–61, 165–70, 177, 188–91; "Mayor Swallow Is City Hall Visitor" (undated newspaper clipping); Cowel interview; Mark Heinz, "Remember the Name: Charles Lewis," *Casper Star-Tribune,* Mar. 8, 2009, A3.

23. Cutrer, "My Boys," 259–60.

24. AS, "Story of a Publisher," 303.

25. Sheila Corley and Frederick Brantley, eds., *Signets: An Anthology of Beginnings* (Baton Rouge, LA: Alan Swallow, Publisher, 1940), 12–13.

26. William Ferris, "An Interview with Cleanth Brooks," *Southern Reader,* Summer 1989, 145.

27. AS, "Story of a Publisher," 304–5; Cutrer, "My Boys," 261–62; Thomas McGrath, *Figures from a Double World* (Denver: Alan Swallow, 1954.

28. Blotner, *Robert Penn Warren,* 65–66; Cutrer, "My Boys," 263; Lincoln Fitzell to AS, Feb. 29, 1940; AS to Lincoln Fitzell, Apr. 1, 1940.

29. Cutrer, "My Boys," 262–63; Raymond Dannenbaum to AS, Mar. 1, 1940.

30. T. M. Pearce to AS, Jan. 17, 1949; AS to RPW, Apr. 12, 1940; RPW to AS, Jan. 3, 1941.

31. "Alan Swallow," *Abstract of Theses* (Baton Rouge: Louisiana State Univ.); Louisiana State University commencement program, June 2, 1941; RPW to AS, Mar. 3, 1941; Lawrence R. Guild, certificate of election to Phi Kappa Phi membership, Aug. 1941.

4: STERN CRITIC

1. Hazel Dreis to AS, undated.

2. AS, "Story of a Publisher," 309; "Some of My Best Friends Are Publishers" (typescript in papers of TA); Hazel Dreis to AS, undated.

3. AS, "Story of a Publisher," 309–10, 312–13; Hermione G. Kilgore to AS, Feb. 19, 1961; J. Richard Phillips, "Alan Swallow, Publisher" (masters thesis, University of New Mexico, Mar. 15, 1963).

4. AS, "Editorial Announcement," and YW, "Three Poems," *Modern Verse,* Jan. 1941, 3–4, 25.

5. AS, "The Swallow Pamphlets," *Modern Verse,* July 1941, back cover.

6. Alan Critchlow, "Two Poems," *Modern Verse,* Oct. 1941, 16–17.

7. Norma N. Yueh, "Alan Swallow, Publisher," *Library Quarterly,* Library of Congress, July 1969, 224.

8. J. V. Cunningham to AS, Aug. 1942.

9. Carol Harper, "Car Hits Dog," *New Mexico Quarterly Review,* 1946, 354–57.

10. AS, "Subjectivism as Poetic Method," *New Mexico Quarterly Review,* 1943, 20.

11. AS, "Man and Woman," *New Mexico Quarterly Review,* 1941, 102–4; "Book Reviews," 241–43; "Poetry," 217–19, also in *NMQR.*

12. AS, literary reviews, *NMQR,* 1942, 366, 496; *NMQR,* 1943, 350; *NMQR,* 1944, 215, 482; *NMQR,* 1945, 76, 216–17; *NMQR,* 1946, 363, 493; *NMQR,* 1948, 456, 461–63.

13. AS, "Allegory as Literary Method," *NMQR,* Aug. 1940, 157; AS to CH, June 1, 1966; M. C. McCrory, "Alan Swallow—Purpose and First Intent," *North American Mentor,* Summer 1967, 5.

14. AS to YW, Oct. 27, 1940.

15. W. O. Clough to AS, Sept. 22, 1940.

16. YW to AS, July 22 and Aug. 10, 1940.

17. AS to YW, Oct. 27, 1940.

18. J. V. Cunningham to AS, Aug. 1, 1942.

19. Lincoln Fitzell to AS, Feb. 20, 1943.

20. Duane Vandenbusche, *The Gunnison Country* (Gunnison, CO: B&B Printers), 431–33; Abbott Fay, *Mountain Academia: A History of Western State College of Colorado* (Boulder, CO: Pruett Press, 1968), 113; MS interview.

21. "Sudden Death of Mrs. Ida K. Swallow" (unidentified newspaper clipping, Sept. 1941); MS interview; "One and One-Half Feet More Snow Than During Winter of Last Year," *Top o' the World,* Mar. 2, 1943, 4.

22. AS, *The Nameless Sight,* 73; Claire, *Publishing in the West,* 18; Robert Brown to AS, Dec. 12, 1942.

23. "Swallow Giggles, Class Undisturbed," *Swallow Squaw (Peep o' de Woild),* May 22, 1943; George Sibley to TA, Jan. 24, year unspecified; MS interview; KS to TA, May 12, 1996.

24. Contract, The Press of James A. Decker, May 1942; undated announcement; Decker to authors, Jan. 29, 1943; Carroll Coleman to AS, Jan. 22, Mar. 29, and Apr. 12, 1943; AS to CH, Jan. 1, 1945; Myron H. Broomell to AS, Feb. 21, 1943.

25. "Writers Workshop Is Very Successful," *Top o' the World* (undated clipping).

26. "Dr. Alan Swallow Joins WSC Team," *Top o' the World,* June 8, 1942, 1, and Sept. 29, 1942, 1, 4.

27. "Wright, Swallow, McClain Leave Western State," *Top o' the World,* Oct. 15, 1943, 1; Cowel interview.

28. E. H. Beneke, memorandum to commanding officer, Nov. 24, 1943; Swallow, "Story of a Publisher," 313; Cowel interview.

29. MS interview; Art Eldridge to Vera Cowel, undated; Associated Press, "Alan Swallow, 51, Publisher, Dead," *New York Times,* Nov. 28, 1966.

30. AS to CH, Feb. 18, 1945.

31. AS to CH, Sept. 19, 1945.

32. MS interview; Cowel interview; Ross Jamieson to AS, Mar. 1966; "Death Summons Virginia Robinson at Billings Hospital" (unidentified clipping); "Virginia Swallow Robinson and Virgil Robinson" (unpublished memo); AS, "First Poems" (unpublished collection, undated).

33. CH to AS, undated; CH to Franklin P. Rolfe, Apr. 8, 1946.

34. Swallow to CH, Nov. 1 and Dec. 13, 1944; Jan. 1, 20, and 26, Feb. 18, June 18, Oct. 19 and 27.

35. Swallow to CH, Nov. 8 and 28, 1945; Feb. 17 and 24, 1946; and June 30, 1958.

5: THE BIGGEST CITY AROUND

1. Cowel interview; David McQuay, "Finally, Denver Pays Tribute to Its Writer's Writer," Sunday Denver Post, Mar. 23, 1967, 34.

2. MS interview; Mark Harris, Short Work of It (Pittsburgh: Pittsburgh Univ. Press), 147; AS to CH, Jan. or Feb. 1946; KS, interview by TA; AS to FW, Feb. 5, 1947.

3. James F. Martin, "A Brief History of the University of Denver Press" (unpublished paper for courses in Research Methods in Librarianship and Literature of Subject Fields, University of Denver, 1954), 2, 10–11; Harry Chrisman, "My Friend, Dr. Alan Swallow: 1915–1966" (unpublished manuscript); Claire, Publishing in the West, 59; James Ryan Morris, "Alan Swallow: Experiment Fulfilled," Mile High Underground, December 1966, 10.

4. Vardis Fisher, interview by John Milton, in "The Western Novel: A Symposium," South Dakota Review, Autumn 1964; VF, "The Western Writer," Western American Literature, Winter 1967, 253.

5. Wallace Stegner, "A Decade of Regional Publishing," Publishers' Weekly, Mar. 11, 1939.

6. McQuay, "Finally, Denver Pays Tribute," 32, 34; John Williams, interview by Jean James, Colorado Libraries, Sept. 1975, 6; Harris, Short Work of It, 149; TA, "Swallow: A Passion to Publish," Colorado Endowment for the Humanities News, Jan. 1992, 3; KS, interviews by TA and by author; AS, "Poet, Publisher and the Tribal

Chant," *Poetry,* Oct. 1949, 48–49; FW, interview by TA, Nov. 1987; Wayne Cornell, interview by author, Aug. 2008.

7. Swallow, "Story of a Publisher," 319; Glenn Clairmonte, *Calamity Was the Name for Jane: The Only Complete Life of Calamity Jane* (Denver: Sage Books, 1959); Edith Eudora Kohl, *Denver's Historic Mansions: Citadels to the Empire Builders* (Denver: Sage Books, 1957); Forbes Parkhill, *The Law Goes West* (Denver: Sage Books, 1956); AS to VF, May 14, 1956.

8. Claire, *Publishing in the West,* 59; John Porter Bloom, minutes of Conference on the History of Western America, Santa Fe, Oct. 12–14, 1961; "Alan Swallow," *Denver Post,* Nov. 27, 1966, 58; Ada Merrill, interview by TA; AS, "Literature of the West Needs No Apology," *Sunday Denver Post,* Feb. 17, 1957, 10; AS to Mr. Roskolenko, Dec. 3, 1950, and Jan. 22, 1951.

9. Claire, *Publishing in the West,* 44; AS to H. W. Reninger, Sept. 29, 1949; Merrill interview.

10. "Pioneer Spotlight," *Bulletin, University of Denver* (undated clipping); Alex Murphree, "Unlimited Horizon for Writers," *Denver Post,* Sept. 30, 1951.

11. Martin, "A Brief History," 11–13.

12. Norman S. Thompson to AS, May 27, 1946; AS to Thompson, Dec. 26, 1947.

13. Charles B. Fahs to AS, Jan. 5, 1948; AS to Fahs, Jan. 8, 1948.

14. AS to John Marshall, undated; Fahs to AS, Jan. 20, 1948.

15. George R. Potter to AS, Jan. 10, 1948; John Marshall to AS, June 8, 1948; AS to Marshall, June 15, 1948.

16. "Death Calls Edgar H. Swallow, Farmer and Businessman" (undated newspaper clipping); AS, "For My Father," *Wyoming Student Verse,* 1937; AS to Fahs, May 23, 1948; Marshall to AS, June 5, 1948; AS to Marshall, June 15, 1948.

17. Milward L. Simpson to AS, May 27, 1948; Cowel interview; "Ansel Emerson Walters Jr." (unpublished manuscript in Swallow Family scrapbook); AS, "Story of a Publisher"; Program, "Fourteenth Annual Honors Banquet," May 28, 1948; AS, "A Message to Friends of Little Mags" (announcement in *Galley's Little Magazine*

184 | Notes to Pages 94–100

Presses, Winter 1949); Claire, *Publishing in the West,* 59–60; Lewis Nichols, "In and Out of Books: Individualist," *New York Times Book Review,* July 16, 1961; Martin Robbins, "Alan Swallow: A Remembrance" (photocopy, source not identified).

18. "Library of Congress Plans Its Second Year of Quarterly Book Lists," *Publishers' Weekly,* Apr. 14, 1945, 1526; George B. Parks, letter to the editor, *Saturday Review,* Mar. 12, 1956, 23; AS, "To the Subscribers for *United States Quarterly Book Review"* (undated announcement); AS, "Story of a Publisher," 325; Vi Gale, interview by TA, undated, and author's email interview, Mar. 19, 2007; Foreword to *The United States Quarterly Book Review,* Mar. 1956; Gus Blaisdell, telephone interview by TA, Sept. 16, 1994.

19. Martin, "A Brief History," 14–16; AS to Janet Lewis, Feb. 6, 1950; Norma N. Yueh, "Alan Swallow, Publisher: 1915–1966," *Library Quarterly,* July 1969, 224–26; AS to FW, Oct. 14, 1948.

20. AS to CH, Feb. 24 and 26, 1946, and Nov. 26, 1955; Hyatt Howe Waggoner to CH, Jan. 4, 1947; AS, "Story of a Publisher," 323; Gale, interview by TA; AS to Allen D. Breck, July 5, 1963, and Aug. 7, 1964.

21. AS, "Story of a Publisher"; "Book Exhibit Features DU Teacher-Publisher," *Rocky Mountain News,* July 3, 1947, 21; Claire, *Publishing in the West,* 58; AS to CH, Sept. 30, 1946, and Jan. 14, 1947; AS to VF, Aug. 28, 1956; AS to FW, Oct. 14, 1948; AS to VF, Aug. 28, 1956, and Dec. 20, 1960.

22. AS to VF, Aug. 28, 1956.

23. Mary Springer, "The Swallow Publishing Adventure," International News Service dispatch, Nov. 4, 1947.

24. AS, "Publishers and Publishing" (undated lecture for Idaho State College Conference).

25. Mark Harris, *Best Father Ever Invented: The Autobiography of Mark Harris* (New York: Dial Press, 1976), 51; AS, "Some Technical Aspects of Recent Poetry," *Western Humanities Review,* Autumn 1952, 346; James Ryan Morris, "Alan Swallow: Experiment Fulfilled," *Mile High Underground,* Dec. 1966, 10.

26. Harris, *Best Father Ever Invented,* 51–52.

27. Dudley Fitts, "Spoiling Crane, Eyeses & Refreshments," *Saturday Review of Literature,* Mar. 1949, 40; Sherman Conrad, "The Common War," *Poetry,* June 1949, 175–77; "Denver Poet: Lyric Notes in Wartime," *Denver Post,* Dec. 1947; Claire, *Publishing in the West,* epigraph.

28. Martin, "A Brief History," 20–22; Bud Mayer, University of Denver press release, Feb. 25, 1954; Robert L. Perkin, "One Man's Pegasus: Agreeable Errand" (Denver newspaper clipping, June 19, 1955); Claire, *Publishing in the West,* 59; AS to VF, Apr. 26, 1952; AS to Opal and Vardis Fisher, Apr. 22, 1955.

6: ALAN SWALLOW, PUBLISHER

1. Claire, *Publishing in the West.*

2. AS to Felix Pollak, Feb. 5, 1962.

3. AS to Dick Elman, Dec. 22, 1960.

4. Claire, *Publishing in the West,* 32–33.

5. AS, "American Publishing and the American Writer," *Chicago Review,* Autumn–Winter 1960, 84.

6. AS, "American Publishing," 97 and 91–92n.

7. J. Richard Phillips, "Alan Swallow, Publisher" (masters thesis, Stanford University, n.d.).

8. Claire, *Publishing in the West,* 30; AS, "Two Contests for Books of Poems" (undated announcement); Vi Gale, *Several Houses* (Denver: Alan Swallow, 1959); Joan Swift, *This Element* (Denver: Alan Swallow, 1965); Nelson Bentley, *Sea Lion Caves* (Denver: Alan Swallow, 1966).

9. AS to VF, Feb. 14, 1957.

10. AS to VF, Mar. 15, 1957; KS to TA, May 12, 1996.

11. AS to VF, Apr. 18, 1957.

12. AS to VF, Mar. 20, 1958.

13. KS, interviews by TA and author; KS to TA, May 12, 1996.

14. John Milton to TA, Aug. 23, 1990.

15. KS, interview by TA; Vi Gale, interview by TA; KS to TA, May 12, 1996.

16. AS to VF, June 4, 1958.

17. AS to VF, Feb. 16, 1958.

18. AS to VF, Jan. 25, 1958.

19. AS to VF, June 4, 1958.

20. AS to VF, June 29, 1958.

21. AS to VF, Aug. 25, 1958.

22. AS to VF, Oct. 28, 1959.

23. AS to VF, Jan. 17 and Mar. 4, 1959.

24. AS to VF, July 4, 1959.

25. KS, interview by TA; AS, "Story of a Publisher," 325.

26. AS to VF, Mar. 26, 1956.

27. AS to VF, Apr. 10, 1956.

28. KS, interview by TA; James Ryan Morris, "Alan Swallow: Experiment Fulfilled," 10, marginal notes in unknown hand.

29. KS, interviews by TA and author.

30. KS, interview by TA.

31. AS to VF, June 4, 1958.

32. KS, interview by TA.

33. AS to VF, June 4, 1958.

34. KS, interviews by TA and author.

35. AS to CH, June 30, 1958; KS, interview by TA.

36. John Holmes, "With Love for Mankind," *New York Times Book Review,* undated clipping.

37. Thomas Hornsby Ferrel, "Ideas and Comment," *Rocky Mountain Herald,* Nov. 24, 1965, 4.

38. AS to Dick Elman, Apr. 29, 1961.

39. AS to Harry Chrisman, Feb. 21, 1964.

40. AS to Dick Elman, Jan. 30, 1961.

41. George A. Cavender to AS, Mar. 16, 1959; Claire, *Publishing in the West,* 70.

42. Claire, *Publishing in the West,* 24, 27.

43. Claire, *Publishing in the West,* 31–32; AS to VF, Nov. 23, 1959.

44. AS to CH, undated.

7: ALAN SWALLOW AND HIS AUTHORS

1. Frank Waters, "Notes on Alan Swallow," *Denver Quarterly,* Spring 1967, 16; Gale, interview by TA, n.d.

2. YW to AS, Sept. 18, 1966.

3. Gale interview by TA, 4.

4. AS to Don Gordon, Aug. 18, 1956, and Jan. 26, 1958.

5. FW, "Of Time and Change: A Memoir" (uncorrected proof, 1988), 12, 2.

6. FW, interview by TA.

7. AS, "A Friendly Word About Our List, New Titles and Some Specials," 1954; Thomas McGrath, *Figures from a Double World* (Denver: Alan Swallow, 1954, jacket copy).

8. AS to Thomas McGrath, Feb. 22, 1964.

9. AS to Mrs. Dorothy Hammond, Apr. 7, 1964.

10. "Alan Swallow, 1915–1966," *Southern Review,* Summer 1967, 796–98.

11. AS, *An Editor's Essays of Two Decades* (Athens: Ohio Univ. Press, 1962), 194–201, and "The Mavericks," 86–88.

12. Gale, interview by TA.

13. AS, *An Editor's Essays,* 334–36.

14. Noel Riley Fitch, *Anaïs: The Erotic Life of Anaïs Nin* (Boston: Little, Brown and Company, 1993), 351–52.

15. Anaïs Nin to Durett Wagner, Dec. 22, 1970.

16. Gunther Stuhlmann, ed., *The Diary of Anaïs Nin, 1955–1966* (New York: Harcourt Brace Jovanovich, 1966), 253–55.

17. Dierdre Bair, *Anaïs Nin: A Biography* (New York: Putnam, 1995), 458.

18. AS to Dick Elman, Apr. 28, 1961; Nin to Felix Pollak, Feb. 4, 1962, with marginal note by Pollak.

19. Gale interview, 5.

20. AS, *An Editor's Essays,* 352; FW, "Of Time and Change," 12.

21. FW interview by TA.

22. AS, *An Editor's Essays,* 353–57.

23. AS to VF, June 30, 1963.

8: VARDIS

1. AS to VF, Apr. 26, 1952.

2. VF to AS, Jan. 16, 1960.

3. AS to VF, Dec. 7, 1965.

4. Opal Fisher to Morton P. Weisman, Oct. 22, 1969.

5. Tim Woodward, "Papers Donated to BSU Paint More Complete Picture of Author," *Idaho Statesman*, June 15, 1997; Frederick Manfred, interview by TA, 142–43.

6. VF, "Vardis Fisher Comments on His 'Testament of Man' Series," *American Book Collector*, Sept. 1963, 36.

7. VF, "A Parable for Librarians on Why Ignorance Is Bliss," *PNLA Quarterly*, Oct. 1939.

8. Ronald W. Taber, "Vardis Fisher and the 'Idaho Guide': Preserving Culture for the New Deal," *Pacific Northwest Quarterly*, Apr. 1968, 68–76.

9. "Dee" to AS, Sept. 28, 1939.

10. Harry W. Schwartz, *Vardis Fisher: A Critical Summary, with Notes on His Life and Personality* (Caldwell, ID: Caxton Printers, 1939, 5–12.)

11. VF to FW, Mar. 6, 1967.

12. AS, interview with VF, *A Way Out*, May–July, 1965, 11–12, and *Inland*, Aug. 1954, 25.

13. AS to Opal and Vardis Fisher, Apr. 22, 1955.

14. VF to AS, May 2, 1955; AS to VF, Aug. 1, 1955.

15. John R. Milton, *Three West: Conversations with Vardis Fisher, Max Evans, Michael Straight* (Vermillion, SD: Dakota Press, 1970).

16. VF to AS, Aug. 5, 1955.

17. VF to AS, Aug. 18, 1955.

18. Claire, *Publishing in the West*, 34.

19. AS to VF, Oct. 29, 1955.

20. AS to VF, Nov. 7, 1955.

21. AS to VF, Feb. 23, 1960.

22. VF to AS, Jan. 16, 1960; AS to VF, Feb. 3, 1960.

23. Opal Laurel Holmes, "Once in a Wifetime," *American Book Collector*, Sept. 1963, 14–15.

24. VF to AS, May 3, 1959.

25. VF to AS, May 7, 1959.

26. George Kellogg, "First Man of Idaho Letters," *A Way Out,* Oct. 1967, 59; Vardis Fisher, *Orphans in Gethsemane* (Denver: Alan Swallow, 1960), photo caption on back jacket.

27. AS to VF, Sept. 5, 1958.

28. AS to VF, June 9, 1960.

29. AS to VF, June 15, 1960.

30. VF to AS, July 14, 1960; AS to VF, July 17, 1960.

31. AS to Caroline Bancroft, Apr. 7, 1962.

32. Tim Woodward, *Tiger on the Road* (Caldwell, ID: Caxton Printers, 1989) 19, 23, 37.

33. Woodward, *Tiger,* 13.

34. AS, "The Mavericks," *Critique: Studies in Modern Fiction,* Winter 1959, 83.

35. AS to VF, July 5, 1966; VF to Ronald Taber, Oct. 29, 1965.

36. AS, "The Mavericks," 83.

37. "Vardis Fisher Week in Idaho," *Idaho Daily Statesman,* Nov. 29, 1962.

38. "Bill" to TA, Feb. 17, 1995.

39. Mick McAllister, "From the Editorial Desk," *Vardis Fisher Newsletter* 1:3.

9: EXPANSION AND COLLAPSE

1. Robert L. Perkin, "It's Denver's Publishing Center," *Rocky Mountain News* (undated clipping).

2. FW, interview by TA, undated.

3. R. C. Gordon-McCutchan, *The Taos Indians and the Battle for Blue Lake* (Santa Fe, NM: Red Crane Books, n.d.), photocopy of foreword by FW, 3.

4. AS to Dick Elman, May 16, 1961.

5. AS, anonymous interview, *Village Voice,* Dec, 1, 1966.

6. Martin Robbins, "Alan Swallow: A Remembrance" (undated photocopy, source not known).

7. Lewis Nichols, "In and Out of Books," *New York Times Book Review,* July 16, 1961; KS, interview by TA; AS to Harry Chrisman, May 1, 1965.

8. AS to VF, May 27, 1960.

9. AS to Harry Chrisman, Apr. 18, 1960.

10. Harry Chrisman to AS, Apr. 21, 1960.

11. AS to Thomas McGrath, Mar. 27, 1962.

12. KS, interview by TA, Jan. 1988.

13. AS to VF, Sept. 1, 1960, with undated handwritten notes by AS; AS to VF, Jan. 12, 1961; AS to Janet Lewis, Sept. 4, 1962.

14. AS to VF, Sept. 9, 1960, and Aug. 21, 1961.

15. AS to VF, Sept. 29, 1963.

16. AS to Harry Chrisman, Sept. 21, year unspecified.

17. AS to Harry Chrisman, Jan. 23, 1962.

18. AS to FW, June 25, year unspecified.

19. Ada Johnson Merrill, interview by TA.

20. AS to Harry Chrisman, Nov. 5, 1962.

21. Edith Shiffert to TA, June 20, 1992.

22. AS to VF, Mar. 27, 1961.

23. VF to unspecified recipient, Feb. 25, 1967.

24. AS to VF, July 27, 1960.

25. AS to FW, June 25, 1961.

26. AS to Thomas McGrath, Aug. 31, 1966.

27. AS to FW, undated; Martha Storm to AS, June 21, 1961, handwritten note on copy of letter.

28. Claire, *Publishing in the West,* 46–48.

29. AS to VF, Mar. 17, 1961.

30. AS to VF, May 19, 1961.

31. AS to VF, Sept. 29, 1961.

32. AS to Dick Elman, Aug. 5, 1962.

33. AS to Harry Chrisman, June 23, 1962; Harry Chrisman to AS, June 26, 1962.

34. AS to Harry Chrisman, Aug. 28, 1962.

35. Isabel Elder to MS, Nov. 25, 1966.

36. AS to Peggy Simpson Curry, Feb. 13, 1961; Peggy Simpson Curry to AS, Feb. 15, 1961.

37. Claire, *Publishing in the West,* 49.

38. AS to VF, Nov. 5, 1960.

39. Newspaper clippings, *Rocky Mountain News,* May 15, 1961, 44, and undated.

40. "One Man's Pegasus: Western Writers," *Rocky Mountain News,* Mar. 19, 1961, 8-A.

41. "Author League Discussion Slated," *Rocky Mountain News,* Nov. 23, 1962, 58.

42. "Colorado Day Essay Judges," photo caption, *Rocky Mountain News,* July 30, 1964, 42.

43. AS to Janet Lewis and YW, July 17, 1964.

44. AS to Janet Lewis, Dec. 2, 1964.

45. Unknown publisher, letter to James Hearst, Aug, 16, 1964.

46. MS, postcard to VF and Opal, Jan. 23, 1963.

47. AS to VF, Feb. 1, 1963.

48. AS to VF, Sept. 8, 1963.

49. AS to VF, Dec. 14, 1963.

50. AS to VF, Apr. 16, 1963.

51. AS to VF, July 10, 1963.

52. AS to VF, Sept. 20, 1963.

53. AS to VF, Jan. 19, 1964.

54. AS to VF, Jan. 19, 1964.

55. AS to George A. Wallis, Jan. 24, 1964.

56. AS to Gus Blaisdell, Jan. 3, 1964, and to Harry Chrisman, Jan. 29, 1965; FW, interview by TA.

57. Claire, *Publishing in the West,* 48–52, 62; AS to CH, June 1 and Oct. 29, 1966.

58. AS to Gus Blaisdell, Nov. 12, 1964, and to Harry Chrisman, Sept. 18 and Oct. 27, 1964.

59. AS to CH, undated.

60. AS to CH, Feb. 13, 1958.

61. AS to CH, Feb. 10, 1958; CH to AS, Feb. 18 and 22, 1958.

62. VF, *Orphans in Gethsemane: A Novel of the Past and Present* (Denver: Alan Swallow, 1960), 209–13.

63. Name withheld to TA, May 12, 1995; AS to "Caroline," Nov. 14, no year given; VF to unidentified recipient, Oct. 29, 1966; VF to Ronald Taber, Dec. 6, 1966.

64. KS, telephone interview by author.

65. AS to CH, Mar. 4, 1965.

66. "Alan Swallow's 26th year 'Sage' Voice from Denver," *Los Angeles Free Press,* Sept. 16, 1966.

67. Vi Gale, interview by TA.

68. AS to VF, undated.

69. AS to VF, Oct. 10, 1965.

70. AS to VF, Oct. 25, 1965.

71. AS to Gus Blaisdell, June 18, 1966.

72. Len Fulton, "In Memoriam: Alan Swallow," *Los Angeles Free Press,* Dec. 23, 1966.

73. AS to CH, Aug. 28, 1965; Feb. 10, Mar. 5, and Oct. 26, 1958; and Oct. 28, 1966, the latter with undated marginal note by CH.

74. Gale, interview by TA; AS to VF, Feb. 24, 1961; KS to TA, May 12, 1996.

75. AS to Harry Chrisman, Sept. 29, 1962.

76. KS, interviews by TS and by author; AS to Thomas McGrath, Aug. 12, 1963; AS to Janet Winters, Mar. 29, May 17, and Aug. 23, 1965.

77. AS to VF, Nov. 3, 1965.

78. AS to VF, Nov. 19, 1965.

79. Gale, interview by TA.

80. Claire, *Publishing in the West,* 51, 56.

81. Opal Fisher to Morton P. Weisman, Oct. 22, 1969.

82. Claire, *Publishing in the West,* 39–40, 51, 53–55; AS to E. K. Damon, Mar. 30, 1965.

83. AS to VF, Jan. 4, 1966.

84. AS to VF, May 31, year not given.

85. AS to VF and Opal, Jan. 4, 1966; Mark Harris, "Alan Swallow, 1915–1966," *University of Denver News,* Dec.–Jan. 1984.

86. AS to Thomas McGrath, Dec. 23, 1965; Harry Chrisman to AS, Nov. 3, 1965.

87. Claire, *Publishing in the West,* 38.

88. AS to Dick Elman, May 14, year not given.

89. Claire, *Publishing in the West,* 31, 36, 48.

90. Claire, *Publishing in the West,* 39, 64–65.

91. VF to FW and Frederick Manfred, Nov. 4, 1967.

92. VF to John Milton, Oct. 22, 1976; VF to Virginia McConnell, undated.

93. Ada Johnson Merrill interview; Roger Hecht to Harry Chrisman, Mar. 17, 1969.

94. FW, interview by TA.

95. VF to FW, Jan. 27, 1966; TA to Virginia McConnell Simmons, Aug. 9, 1990; Simmons to TA, Aug. 30, 1990; W. Dale Nelson to Simmons, Sept. 25, 2007.

96. AS, "For Mae," *The Nameless Sight: Poems 1937–1956* (Denver: Swallow Paperbooks, 1956), 45.

97. VF, memo to Frederick Manfred, Nov. 22, 1967.

98. Isabel Elder to MS, Nov. 25, 1966; AS to FW, June 8, 1966.

99. YW, "Alan Swallow, 1915–1966," *Southern Review,* Summer 1967.

100. AS to CH, Oct. 29, 1966.

101. CH to her family, Nov. 27, 1966.

102. Carolyn Bancroft to MS, Nov. 29, 1966; Olga Curtis, "The Battling Historians," *Empire Magazine,* Jan. 16, 1972.

103. FW interview.

104. YW, "Alan Swallow," *Southern Review,* 978.

105. Henry A. Clausen to FW, Dec. 5, 1967.

106. Marie and Scott Broom, note to Cathy and Harry Chrisman, Nov. 26, 1966.

107. Mark Harris, "Obituary Three for Alan Swallow," *Modern Fiction Studies,* Summer 1969, 189.

108. CH, handwritten marginal note dated Sept. 21, 1990, on typed letter, CH to AS, Oct. 18, 1966.

109. CH to Morton Weisman, June 4, 1975.

110. KS to TA, May 12, 1996.

10: POSTMORTEM

1. Ralph Elder to MS, Nov. 24, 1966.

2. Vi Gale interview.

3. Thomas Hornsby Ferril, "Ideas and Comment," *Rocky Mountain Herald,* Dec. 3, 1966.

4. University of Denver announcement, undated.

5. VF to FW, Jan. 27, 1966.

6. VF to Dick Elman, Dec. 15, 1966.

7. John R. Little to Harry Chrisman, Mar. 1, 1968.

8. KS, telephone interview by author.

9. "Memorial Rites for Dr. Swallow at DU on Saturday" (undated newspaper clipping); Morris, "Alan Swallow: Experiment Fulfilled," AS, *The Nameless Sight,* 11.

10. CH to family, Nov. 27, 1966.

11. Maurice and Carol Harper, night letter to MS, Nov. 27, 1966.

12. VF to MS, Nov. 27, 1966.

13. YW to MS, Nov. 26, 1966.

14. Harry Chrisman to Martin Miller, Dec. 1, 1966; Miller to Chrisman, Jan. 10, 1968; Chrisman to MS, Jan. 11, 1968.

15. CH to Bob Rawls, Dec. 2, 1966, with copy of postcard, AS to CH, undated.

16. Roger Hecht to MS, Dec. 15, 1966.

17. MS and Gus Blaisdell to "friends and authors," Jan. 13, 1967, misdated as 1966.

18. VF to FW, Jan. 13, 1967.

19. MS to FW and Frederick Manfred, Jan. 23, 1967.

20. VF to Ronald W. Taber, May 7, 1967.

21. Dick McBush to Gus Blaisdell, Mar. 14, 1967.

22. Virginia McConnell to Martin Miller, Jan. 10, 1967.

23. Thomas McGrath to MS, undated; Willard A. Lockwood to Gus Blaisdell, Dec. 23, 1966.

24. Harry Kaste to MS, Apr. l9, 1967.

25. Stanton Peckham, "Reader's Roundup," *Denver Post* (undated clipping).

26. MS to "authors and friends," undated.

27. Gus Blaisdell, interview by TA.

28. Van Allen Bradley, "New Publishing House Here," *Daily News,* Feb. 23, 1969; Donna Ippolito and Shirley Kopatz, "Alan

Swallow: Platen Press Publisher," *Journal of the West,* July, 1969, 481–83.

29. "Author of 'Ladder of Rivers'" to MS, Aug. 7, 1967; Stanton Peckham, "Reader's Roundup," *Sunday Denver Post,* Aug. 6, 1967, 13, and May 28, 1967, with marginal note by Chrisman.

30. Stanton Peckham, "Reader's Roundup," *Sunday Denver Post,* Aug. 6, 1967.

31. Vi Gale interview.

32. Ada Johnson Merrill interview.

33. Durett Wagner to Swallow authors, Dec. 13, 1968.

34. Durett Wagner to VF, Sept. 25, 1967.

35. Robert S. Robin to Martin Miller, Aug. 30, 1967.

36. Durett Wagner to VF, Sept. 25, 1967.

37. VF, typed note at bottom of Wagner's Sept. 25 letter.

38. VF to Morton P. Weisman, Aug. 7, 1967.

39. John Milton to Durett Wagner, June 6, 1970.

40. Frederick Manfred to FW, Dec. 4, 1967.

41. Martin Miller to FW, Oct. 27, 1967.

42. VF to Delbert E. Wylder, Nov. 18, 1967.

43. John Milton to VF and Opal, Oct. 19, 1967.

44. TA to Virginia Simmons, Aug. 9, 1990.

45. VF, unsigned letter to John Milton, Oct. 22, 1967.

46. Caroline Bancroft to VF, Nov. 20, 1967; Ada Johnson Merrill interview.

47. VF to Martin P. Weisman, Dec. 23, 1966, and May 9, 1967.

48. Stanton Peckham, "Reader's Roundup" (undated clipping).

49. Stanton Peckham, "Reader's Roundup," *Sunday Denver Post,* Oct. 22, 1967; Hoke Norris, "Chicago," *Chicago Sun-Times Book Week,* Nov. 19, 1967.

50. Durett Wagner to Virginia McConnell, Dec. 20, 1967.

51. Thomas McGrath to Morton P. Weisman, undated.

52. Virginia McConnell to Durett Wagner, Nov. 25, 1967; Wagner to McConnell, Dec. 20, 1967.

53. VF to Martin P. Miller, Nov. 18.

54. Martin Miller to Durett Wagner, Feb. 18, 1970; Wagner to Miller, Apr. 23, 1970.

55. Morton Weisman, proposal, Nov. 5, 1973.

56. Morton Weisman to Francis Wolle, May 2, 1977.

57. Morton Weisman to Swallow authors, undated.

58. Claire, *Publishing in the West,* 41.

59. William Hogan, "A Tribute to the Late Publisher Alan Swallow" (undated clipping from San Francisco newspaper).

60. KS to TA, Sept. 7, 1987.

61. Ross Jamieson to TA, March, 1996.

Bibliography

ARCHIVES, UNPUBLISHED MANUSCRIPTS,
INTERVIEWS

Archives

Auer, Thomas M., collected papers
Bird Library, Syracuse University
The Clore Collection of Vardis Fisher Materials, Special Collections Department, Boise State University
Photo Archives, Stanford University News Service
Robert Penn Warren Library, Western Kentucky University
University of New Mexico Center for Southwest Studies
U.S. Department of the Interior, homesteading documents
William Robertson Coe Library, University of Wyoming

Unpublished Manuscripts in Papers of Thomas M. Auer

Clough, Wilson. "Alan Swallow as Poet." Undated.
Gruson, Gene De. "E. Haldeman-Julius." Speech for Tri-State Craftsmen's Club, May 6, 1991.
McCracken, Kenneth Donald. "E. Haldeman-Julius: A Critical Evaluation." Thesis, Kansas State Teachers College, May 1956.
Montesi, Albert Joseph. "The *Southern Review* (1935–1942): A History and Evaluation." Dissertation, Pennsylvania State Univ., Aug. 1955.

Phillips, J. Richard. "Alan Swallow, Publisher." Thesis, not otherwise identified, Mar. 15, 1963.

Swallow, Alan, ed. "A New Poetry: An Anthology, 1934–37."

———. "Some of My Best Friends Are Publishers." Typescript.

Interviews

Cowel, Vera, by Thomas M. Auer, Fort Collins, CO, 1987.

Gale, Vi, by Thomas M. Auer, undated.

Sestak, Joseph, by author, Laramie, WY, Sept. 30, 2005.

Staver, Ronald T., by author, Sept. 19, 2005.

Swallow, Karen, by Thomas M. Auer, Portland, OR, Jan. 1988.

Swallow, Karen, telephone interview by author, Mar. 9, 2006.

Swallow, Mae, by Thomas M. Auer, Denver, Sept. 26, 1987.

Waters, Frank, by Thomas M. Auer, Nov. 1987.

BOOKS AND ARTICLES

Anderson, Lenore. "Haldeman-Julius: Little Blue Books 50th Anniversary." *American Book Collector,* Apr.–May 1969.

Bair, Deirdre. *Anaïs Nin: A Biography.* New York: Putnam, 1995.

Barth, R. L., ed. *The Selected Letters of Yvor Winters.* Athens: Swallow Press/Ohio Univ. Press, 2000.

Blaisdell, Gus. "He Breathes Another Air· Alan Swallow." *Author & Journalist,* Mar. 1963.

Blotner, Joseph. *Robert Penn Warren: A Biography.* New York: Random House, 1997.

Chickering, Sharon K. "Great Escapes: Leadville." *Denver Post,* Aug. 3, 1997.

Claire, William F., ed. *Publishing in the West: Alan Swallow, Some Letters and Commentaries.* Santa Fe: The Lightning Tree, 1974.

Conkin, Paul K. *The Southern Agrarians*. Knoxville: Univ. of Tennessee Press, 1988.

Corley, Sheila, and Frederick Brantley, eds. *Signets: An Anthology of Beginnings*. Baton Rouge, LA: Alan Swallow, Publisher, 1940.

Coumbe, Arthur T., and Lee S. Harford. *U.S. Army Cadet Command: The 10-Year History*. Fort Monroe, VA: Office of the Command Historian, U.S. Army Cadet Command, 1996.

Cutrer, Thomas W. *Parnassus on the Mississippi: The* Southern Review *and the Baton Rouge Literary Community, 1935–1942*. Baton Rouge: Louisiana State Univ. Press, 1984.

"Death Calls Edgar A. Swallow, Powell Farmer and Business Man." *Powell Tribune*, Apr. 27, 1948.

Elman, Richard. "A Publisher for Poets." *Saturday Review*, July 22, 1961.

Fay, Abbott. *Mountain Academia: A History of Western State College of Colorado*. Boulder, CO: Pruett Press, 1968.

Ferris, William. "An Interview with Cleanth Brooks." *Southern Reader: A Preview of Current Books on Southern History and Culture*, Summer 1989.

Fisher, Vardis. "A Parable for Librarians on Why Ignorance Is Bliss." *PNLA Quarterly*, Oct. 1939.

———. "Vardis Fisher Comments on His 'Testament of Man' Series." *American Book Collector*, Sept. 1963.

Harmatz, Herb. "Alan Swallow Has Printer's Ink in His Blood; Sets by Hand." Louisiana State Univ. publication, May 16, 1940.

Hensley, Marcia Meredith. *Staking Her Claim: Women Homesteading the West*. Glendo, WY: High Plains Press, 2008.

Holmes, Opal Laurel. "Once in a Wifetime." *American Book Collector*, Sept. 1963.

Hume, Martha M. "A Big Man Goes Down." *Small Press Review*, Spring 1967.

Ippolito, Donna, and Shirley Kopatz. "Alan Swallow: Platten Press Publisher." *Journal of the West,* July 1967.

Johnstone, Jane. "From Saltsage to Security: A Settlement Is Born, Takes Root and Grows to Become a Thriving Wyoming Community." Powell, WY: N.p., 1909, 1959.

Kellogg, George. "First Man of Idaho Letters." *A Way Out,* Oct. 1967.

Koelling, Robert. *First National Bank of Powell: The History of a Bank, a Community, and a Family.* Powell, WY: First National Bank of Powell, 1997.

Larson, Daro. "Churches Establish Moral Tone: 17 Denominations Represented in Town of High Morality." Powell, WY: N.P., 1909–1959.

Larson, T. A. *History of Wyoming.* Lincoln: Univ. of Nebraska Press, 1965.

"LSU Resumes Publication of Its Distinguished Literary Journal." *LSU Outlook,* Jan. 1965.

McConnell, Virginia. "Alan Swallow and Western Writers." *South Dakota Review,* Summer 1967.

McCrory, M. C. "Alan Swallow—Purpose and First Intent." *North American Mentor,* Summer 1967.

McGrath, Thomas. *Figures from a Double World.* Denver: Alan Swallow, 1954.

Metz, Jerred. *The Last Eleven Days of Earl Durand.* Glendo, WY: High Plains Press, 2005.

Morris, James Ryan. "Alan Swallow: Experiment Fulfilled." *Mile High Underground,* Dec. 1966.

Robbins, Martin. "Alan Swallow: A Remembrance." Photocopy, unidentified source.

Ryan, William F. "In Search of Haldeman Julius." *American Rationalist,* Sept.–Oct. 1973.

Scott, Mark. "The Little Blue Books in the War on Bigotry and Bunk." *Kansas History,* Autumn 1978.

Stafford, Jean. "Some Letters to Peter and Eleanor Taylor." *Shenandoah,* Spring 1979.

Stegner, Wallace. "A Decade of Regional Publishing." *Publishers' Weekly,* Mar. 11, 1939.

Swallow, Alan. "Allegory as Literary Method." *New Mexico Quarterly Review,* 1943, 20.

———. "The Careful Young Men." *The Nation,* Mar. 9, 1957.

——— (under the pseudonym e. cummings e.). "Derelict." *Sage: A Literary Journal,* Oct. 1933.

———. "Editorial Announcement." *Modern Verse,* Jan. 1941.

———. "Hart Crane: A Second Quest." *Sage,* Jan. 1934.

———. "The Mavericks." *Critique: Studies in Modern Fiction,* Winter 1959.

———. *The Nameless Sight: Poems 1937–1956.* Denver: Swallow Paperbooks, 1956.

———. "On Reading and Writing." *Sunday Denver Post,* Jan. 20, 1957.

———. "Story of a Publisher." *New Mexico Quarterly Review,* Winter 1966–67.

———. "Subjectivism as Poetic Method." *New Mexico Quarterly Review,* 1943.

———. *Two Stories.* Denver: Alan Swallow, Publisher, 1953.

Taber, Ronald W. "Vardis Fisher and the 'Idaho Guide': Preserving Culture for the New Deal." *Pacific Northwest Quarterly,* Apr. 1968.

Tebbel, John. *Between Covers.* New York: Oxford Univ. Press, 1987.

Twelve Southerners. *I'll Take My Stand: The South and the Agrarian Tradition.* New York: Peter Smith, 1951.

Underwood, Thomas A. *Allen Tate: Orphan of the South.* Princeton, NJ: Princeton Univ. Press, 2000.

Vandenbusche, Duane. *The Gunnison Country.* Gunnison, CO: B&B Printers, n.d.

Warren, Robert Penn. *New and Selected Essays.* New York: Random House, 1989.

Waters, Frank. *Of Time and Change.* Advance uncorrected proof, 1998.

Winters, Yvor. *The Function of Criticism: Problems and Exercises.* Denver: Alan Swallow, 1957.

Woolcott, Alexander. "After June 30, the Deluge." *New Yorker,* June 20, 1925.

Yueh, Norma M. "Alan Swallow, Publisher." *Library Quarterly,* July 1969, 224.

Index

Page numbers in italics denote illustrations.

American Civil Liberties Union,
99, 111–12, 147, 157
Anderson, Sherwood, 27
Auden, W. H., 32, 64
Auer, Thomas M., 165

Bentley, Nelson, 104
Berryman, John, 64
Big Mountain Press, 61, 67
Blaisdell, Gus, 92–93, 160
Branding Iron, The (student newspaper), 34, 37
Brooks, Cleanth, 45, 47–48, 50
Byron, George Gordon, 27

Caxton Printers (later Caxton
Press), 16, 84, 129
Chrisman, Harry, 149–50, 159–60
Ciardi, John, 64
Cody, William F. (Buffalo Bill),
3–4
Crane, Arthur G., 37, *38*

Crane, Hart, 30, 31
Critchlow, Horace, 61, 62, 67,
84, 92
Cunningham, J. V., 62
Curry, Peggy Simpson, 32

Davidson, Donald, 43, 45
Decker, James A., 71, 100
Denver, 81
Denver Post (newspaper), 162
Durand, Earl, 51–54
Dworshak, Henry, 127–28

Eberhart, Richard, 32, 64
Elder, Isabel, 19
Elder, Ralph, 19, 155
Experiment (magazine), 62–63, 78

Farrell, James T., 85
Ferril, Thomas Hornsby, 111, 155–56
Fisher, Opal, 123, 151

Fisher, Vardis, *124;* article about AS planned, 159; childhood, 123; *Children of God* (book), 127; earnings, 55, 127, 128, 158, 165; first publication by AS, 61; *Goat for Azazel* (book), 126–27; home in Hagerman, 33–34; and *Idaho Guide* (book) literary reputation, 119, 124–29; *In Tragic Life* (book), 30–31; *Jesus Came Again* (book), 126; *Love and Death* (book), 127; meets AS, 123; and Virginia McConnell, 151, 164–65; *Mountain Man* (book), 129–30; *Orphans in Gethsemane* (book), 127–28, 154; personality, 123–24; political views, 129–30; research of, 118, 125–26; on sale of AS's publishing business, 158–59, 160–61, 166; similar background to AS, 123; on AS memorial, 156; Mae Swallow's view of, 135; *Tale of Valor* (book), 127–28; *Testament of Man* (series of books), 125, 129; *Tiger on the Road* (biography of), 129

Fitzell, Lincoln, 57, 60, 62

Fugitive, The (magazine), 43–44

Gale, Vi: and death of AS, 155; *Love Always* (book), 118; meets AS, 117–18; and Anaïs Nin, 121; on sale of AS's press, 162; on AS, 114

Gawthrop, Johnny, 54

Gordon, Don, 115

Grand Canyon of the Colorado, 16–17

Graves, Frank Pierrepont, 38–39

Haldeman-Julius, Emanuel, 14–16, 44

Hansen, Clifford, 34, 36–37

Harcourt, Brace and World, 125–26, 166–67

Harper, Carol Ely: and death of AS, 157–58; first publication by AS, 62–63; in Pasco, 80; poems and correspondence, 62–63, 77; suggests newspaper job for AS, 80

Harper Prize, 128

Harris, Joel Chandler, 41

Harris, Mark, 98, 99

Heart Mountain, 9, *11*

Homestead Act, 1–3

Humphries, Rolfe, 156

Idaho Daily Statesman (newspaper), 129

I'll Take My Stand (book), 41–43, 45

Jamieson, Ross, 17, 20–21, 26, 168

Johnson, Raymond, 87, *93,* 135–36

Kirk, Gardner, 44

Knopp, Emil, 52–53

Laramie Republican-Boomerang
(newspaper), 51
Leadville, Colorado, and Southern Railroad, 1, *2*
Lewis, Janet, 94, *105, *118–19
Lewis and Clark College, 146–47
Little Blue Books, 15–16, 44
Long, Huey, 46
Louisiana State University, 46

Manfred, Frederick, 118, 122, 163
McConnell, Virginia, 151, 160–61, 164–65
McGrath, Thomas, 36, 57, 62
Miller, Martin, 160–61
Mills, Clark, 40
Milton, John, 163–64
Murphree, Alex, 87

New Masses (magazine), 26–27
New Mexico Quarterly Review (magazine), 62, 74
Nin, Anaïs, 119–21

Olson, Ted, 30, 51, 58

Pedigo, Bill, 28
Peters, Hazel, 19
Poetry (magazine), 100–101
Pole, Rupert, 119–20
Powell, John Wesley, 7–8

Powell Grade School, 10–11
Powell Powwow (school newspaper), 18, 21

Ransom, John Crowe, 43, 45, 72
Reclamation Act of 1902, 1–3
Reserve Officers Training Corps, 24, 37–38
Robinson, Mrs. Charles, 2
Roosevelt, Franklin D., 24, 34
Rubaiyat of Omar Khayyam, The, 16

Sage (campus literary magazine), 28, 30–31
Sage Books, 61, 86
Shiffert, Edith, 104
Shorey, Madolin, 28–31
Shoshone Reclamation Project, 3–5
Southern Agrarians, 31, 43–44
Southern Review, The (magazine), 46–47
Stafford, Jean, 47
Stafford, William, 147
Stagecoach (movie), 52
Stegner, Wallace, 84
Stevens, Wallace, 64
Stribling, T. S., *42*
Swallow, Alan, *8, 10, 88, 107, 133;* and airplanes, 33–34; alcohol, 109; appearance, 19, 78; on W. H. Auden, 64; automobiles, 9, 13–14, 15, 17, 22–23, 30, 33, *106,* 106–7, 108; baseball, 107;

Swallow, Alan (*cont.*)
basketball, 107–8; on John
Berryman, 63–64; birth, 6–7;
businessman, 79–80, 135, 139,
153, 165–62; on John Ciardi,
64; college, 39, *39*; critic, 27,
30–31, 63–65, 93–94, 142–43;
death, 154; debate, 21, 34,
37, 73; Denver home, 81–82,
83; at Denver University, 82;
with Denver University Press,
88; described by colleagues,
65; described by self, 78, 80,
113; early reading, 8, 9–10;
on Richard Eberhart, 64; as
editor, 28–32, 34, 37, 51, 72,
74; in elementary school,
10–11; on T. S. Eliot, 63–64;
and farming, 9, *12;* as father,
110; fatherly advice to, 21,
29; on William Faulkner, 45;
fellowships, 46; on female
writers, 134–35; first book
of poems *(The Remembered
Land),* 71; first poems, 17–20,
29–30, 33–34, 35; and Vardis
Fisher, 123–30, 151, 156–59;
"For Mae" (poem), 151–52;
as freshman, 25; on Robert
Frost, 64; and Vi Gale, 114,
117–18; and Haldeman-Julius,
15–16, 44; and Carol Ely
Harper, 62–63, 77–78, 84–85,
96, 142–43, 153; health, 91,
94, 98–99, 106–7, 137, 138,
139, 140, 141–42, 145, 149;

high school commencement,
21–23, *22;* horseracing, 106–7;
Laramie apartment, 34; and
Janet Lewis, 94, 118–19; and
Louisiana, 44, 48; and Frederick Manfred, 122; marriage,
32–33; memorial, 156; military
service, 73–79, *76;* motorcycles, 9, 17, 108; *The Nameless
Sight* (book), 111; nickname,
20–21; and Anaïs Nin, 119–21;
overseas publishing, 97;
payment of authors, 95; pen
name, 35; poetry reviewed,
100–101, 111; politics, 26, 66,
111–12; postwar years, 97; on
Ezra Pound, 64; as publisher,
65–66, 95–99, *93,* 102, 114,
122; on publishers, 65–66; and
religion, 13, 109; and ROTC,
24, 38; and Southern Agrarians, 41; sports, 21; on Wallace
Stevens, 64; in Student League
for Industrial Democracy, 36;
and Karen Swallow, 146–47;
and Mae (Elder) Swallow, *33,*
74–75; and Allen Tate, 118–19;
teaching, 58–59, 66, 82, 88,
90, 99, 131; on Dylan Thomas,
63–64; on vanity publishing,
95; and Robert Penn Warren,
49–50, 64; and Frank Waters,
121, 132; on William Carlos
Williams, 64; wins poetry
prize, 34–35; and Yvor Winters, 62, 114, 117

Swallow, Edgar, Jr.: in business, 29; as churchgoer, 13; death of, 90; as farmer, 5, 12–13, *12, 13;* as father, 7, 21, 22–23; homesteading, 5; marriage, 6; military service, 75, *76*

Swallow, Edgar, Sr., 1–3, *2, 4*

Swallow, Ida Kate, 2–5, *4*

Swallow, Karen, *69, 70, 107;* behavior as child, 81–82; 85; birth of, 68–69; correspondence of, 109–10; and Janet Lewis, 85; poem to, 69–70; and Powell, 40; and religion, 109; on AS, 106–7, 110, 144–45, 154

Swallow, Mae (Elder), *33, 69, 83, 107;* and airplanes, 33; at business school, 32; drinking rumors, 151; employment, 47, 103; health, 151; jealousy, 152; marriage, 32–33; and Virginia McConnell, 160–61; on Powell, 47; sale of publishing business, 161–62; meets AS, 19

Swallow, Vera, 7, *10, 91*

Swallow, Virginia, 5, *10,* 75

Sweetland, Monroe, 36

Swift, Joan, 104

Tate, Allen, 43, 45, 118–19

Triem, Eve, 145

Understanding Fiction (book), 55

Understanding Poetry (book), 55

University of Denver, 82–101

University of New Mexico, 60–67

University of Wyoming, 24–40; fraternities, 24; ROTC, 24, 38; AS majors in English, 25

Vanderbilt University, 40, 46

Wagner, Durett, 161–62, 163, 166–67

Warren, Robert Penn, *42;* "The Briar Patch" (essay), 41–43; on Janet Lewis, 118–19; poems criticized by AS, 49–50; at *Southern Review,* 46; on AS's poetry, 40

Waters, Frank, *116;* on eastern publishers, 84; family background, 121; *The Man Who Killed the Deer* (book), 121; *Pumpkin Seed* (book), 165–66; and student manuscripts, 87; and Mae Swallow, 153

Wayne, John, 52

Weisman, Morton, 161–62, 167

Western (Colorado) State College, 67–72

Winters, Yvor, *105;* Bollingen Prize for *Collected Poems,* 131; criticism of AS's poetry, 116; editing by AS, 114; *Forms of Discovery* (book), 165–66;

Winters, Yvor (*cont.*)
as printer, 66; publication by
AS, 54, 108; reviewed by AS,
63; urges AS to abandon publishing, 66–67

Woodward, Tim, 129

Yale Series of Younger Poets, 30
Yellowstone National Park, 14, 17